Noble Intent

Be noble, and the nobleness
that lies in other men,
sleeping but never dead,
will rise in majesty to meet
thine own.

-James Russell Lowell

Noble Intent

Published by Indaba Press & Morgan James Publishing
Indaba, Inc.
Treasure Island, FL 33706-1105
727-360-0111
www.Indaba1.com
www.21Laws.com
www.NobleIntent.com

ISBN: 978-1-58570-403-3

Printed in the United States of America.

Distributed in the United States by Ingram Publishing Services.

Contents

Foreward

by General Paul E. (Gene) Blackwell
and Dennis Barko

When Hellen Davis first told me about a new value system she called Noble Intent, I can honestly say I wasn't exactly sure what she was talking about. But knowing Hellen as well as I do, and judging by her level of enthusiasm, I figured Noble Intent was destined to become the next step in the evolution of executive coaching.

I was wrong. Noble Intent, you see, is less of an evolution and more of a revolution in business philosophy. Indeed, as a value system, Noble Intent has the potential to reach far beyond corporate corridors, and change - for the better - the way people interact.

Noble Intent is based on the belief that people, given the proper circumstances, will always perform nobly and exceed expectations. As a value system, it requires that the practitioner both acts with Noble Intent towards others, and assumes other people have Noble Intent. Consequently, someone practicing Noble Intent will never knowingly do anything purposefully harmful to another.

In that sense, there is almost something spiritual about Noble Intent. It is the antidote for today's world, rife with cynicism and distrust of others. Just think how much easier conducting business (and your life) will be once you replace those dual negatives with the positives of personal ethics and a belief in others.

Hellen's belief in others makes her the ideal person to write about Noble Intent. Along with being among the most outgoing, positive people I know, she has an impressive understanding of what it takes to be a successful corporate leader in America. But most important, she deeply believes in people and their desire to make a difference.

If you want to make a difference in your business (or life), I urge you to read this book. I can't think of a profession (or person) who will not benefit from practicing the tenets of Noble Intent. From members of Congress, to parents and children, adopting a value system of Noble Intent will lead to trust, understanding and a higher plane of commitment. In short, Noble Intent will change the way we view each other.

- General Gene Blackwell

The first time I heard the phrase Noble Intent was the day I started working for Fran Landolf at the Agency in 2001. I was familiar with the concept, but Fran was the first person to give the value system a name. Perhaps more important, he demonstrated the power of Noble Intent every day in the way he managed our organization and lived his life.

As a leader, Fran used Noble Intent as the foundation for every decision he made - and Fran was not adverse to making decisions or accepting responsibility. As leader of our organization, he established a set of values that centered on acting with, and assuming Noble Intent.

Noble Intent's one-two punch was tested regularly at the Agency. In fact, it wasn't at all unusual during the course of a day for someone, somewhere in the enterprise to render a decision that was at once perplexing and irritating. The first instinct for most people in our group was to complain. But Fran never joined the chorus. Instead, he tamped down the moaning, always suggesting that there was probably a good reason for a decision and that we should find out what it was.

Watching Fran practice Noble Intent convinced me that it was the way I wanted to live. Today, Noble Intent plays a huge part in my life. Every time someone does something that I find confounding, I hear Fran's voice reminding me to assume Noble Intent and not jump to conclusions. Next thing I know, I'm on the phone asking that person to explain their reasoning. And because of Fran, I also act with Noble Intent, putting the good of the overall enterprise first.

Fran has retired from the Agency. Yet his name is still synonymous with Noble Intent in our organization. So it is not surprising that he has coauthored a book on this truly important and enlightened value system. Take it from me, you couldn't learn about Noble Intent from a better man.

- Dennis Bartko

Free Noble Intent!

Like the cartoons in Noble Intent? Want them delivered for free right to your computer? Click on **Noble Intent Cartoons** on the Indaba website to select your free gifts including:

•Noble Intent Posters   •Cartoons   •Computer Backgrounds
•Screensavers   •Self-talk handouts   •Introductory Videos
•Noble Intent eZines*   •Book Excerpts

INDABA

For information on eTraining and other products Indaba has to offer, please visit

www.indaba1.com

Email: info@indaba1.com

*eZines are short educational seminars delivered in video, audio or paper format. Each session is designed to give the viewer a basic, yet important, knowledge of the topic at hand. While the information learned is of extremely high value, we deliver all eZines to you for free.

Introduction
The Noble Intent Domino Effect

Chain reactions can result from good or bad behaviors.

We were working with an executive team in Chicago that had serious issues and antagonism so deep seated that some of the issues seemed irresolvable. No one would budge from their fortified positions. What made the situation even more frustrating was that we knew these executives were genuinely good, smart people who were just behaving poorly.

Before meeting with the executive team, we strategized about how best to get them to realize that the effects of their actions were hurting the organization. Fran listened intently to the background of the organization and stories about how peers in this group treated each other disrespectfully, discourteously and had acted with malice.

After thinking for a few minutes, Fran said, "Hellen, these people are not acting nobly. They are not acting with Noble Intent. They also don't think that their peers' intentions are good. Trust has been destroyed. We really need to talk to them about acting with and assuming Noble Intent."

So we decided that Fran should enlighten the group on the concepts of "Noble Intent". Over the following days, we fleshed out the concept of Noble Intent so that Fran was solid in his delivery of this important message to this group. And so Noble Intent was born.

The good news is that Fran's talk to this executive team solidified our belief in our Noble Intent hypothesis. The core of team members instantly saw that Noble Intent was a principle that they thought would help them behave like leaders. They made a decision to commit - as a team and individually - to the tenets of acting with Noble Intent and assuming Noble Intent in their day-to-day interactions for the benefit of their organization.

Fran and I celebrated over lunch. As we were enjoying our meal, one of the executives came over and told us that he had changed his schedule so that he could stay and spend more time talking about Noble Intent with his peers. He confessed that he was contemplating resigning from the organization prior to the meeting, but was energized by the prospect that the organization's leadership was making a commitment to interacting in a noble manner. The executive felt re-energized by the potential results of this concept. He wanted to give the organization a bit more time - a chance to behave nobly. He yearned for a culture built on the foundation of Noble Intent. The exec was particularly excited because his peers all stated their commitment to the concept, and agreed to interact in that manner. After our meeting, he said that he now had hope that the executive team could work as it should - for the good of the organization, peers, employees and stakeholders. He was very emotional, and Fran and I were feeling pretty good about his Noble Intent talk!

There was no question in our minds that people needed to learn about Noble Intent. As we talked and discussed what happens in organizations when people choose to behave poorly, we found ourselves coming back to two basic beliefs: People are, with rare exceptions, inherently good, and that they typically choose to do what is right and what is noble. Based on these beliefs, it isn't too much of a stretch to assume that the majority of people also act with Noble Intent. So, in the majority of situations we would be wise to first assume Noble Intent in our dealings with people - in our relationships. Combined, these tenets formed the foundation upon which we build the Principles of Noble Intent.

Fran and Hellen saw examples of people going against the Noble Intent principles in our work every day. Maybe we could actually start to make people think twice about doing things that we viewed as ignoble, shameful, improper, unethical or dishonorable. Maybe people would think twice about doing the wrong things - things they normally wouldn't do if they had the time to think through the consequences properly. Maybe we could explain Noble Intent so that people would change their actions and thinking, and do the things they should be doing - instead of things they thought were okay for the circumstance they were currently in. And maybe we could get people to overcome the tendency to attribute perceived failings of others to their character, while attributing their own personal failings to their environment. Maybe - just maybe - we could get people to open up and trust each other again by setting up the framework for Noble Intent relationships.

We truly believed that if people understood the concept of acting with and assuming Noble Intent, they would realize its value. This, of course, made us resolve to spread the Noble Intent message to other organizations. Our next problem was getting the message out. We are passionate about the message, and think the concept is important for organizations. Moreover, people need to understand that what they do every day - no matter how insignificant the action may seem - does make a difference. In fact, each choice we make or action we take is like toppling the lead domino in a string of dominoes. When you push over a strategically positioned domino, you can make thousands of other dominoes drop in order. We've seen domino rallies filmed by the media. People are always amazed at the effect one little domino has at setting in motion the other tens of thousands in the chain; the reaction is simply known as the "Domino Effect."

In life, the energy we release can set in motion actions and behaviors in others. In that sense, Noble Intent is analogous to the "domino effect." The things you do - intentionally or unintentionally, nobly or ignobly, right or wrong - can set powerful forces in motion. We have an effect - positive or negative - on everyone we touch, just like the domino effect.

NOBLER: One who acts with and assumes Noble Intent

Organizations function much like a chain of dominoes. Imagine that the lines of dominoes in the diagram are people in your organization. The string is brimming with potential energy that can be released in different ways. How the dominoes drop and release their energy depends on several factors, from political, procedural and influential, to process and strategy. The effect each domino (person) will have on the chain depends on the potential energy stored in their personal and positional power. When a force is introduced, the dominoes tumble - their potential energy is discharged - and effects are felt by the dominoes down the line. Remember, if you've ever played with dominoes - it can be positive or negative. I certainly remember cursing when they fell the wrong way and ruined my plan!

For Noble Intent to succeed, Noblers must exert more impact over the organization than the non-Noblers. How many dominoes from Noblers and non-Noblers fall will correlate to the amount of power in play from you and others with whom you have aligned. You and those aligned with you may knock over all, some, or none of the dominoes.

The fight for the Principles of Noble Intent plays out at every organizational level and on multiple fields. So you must have a plan to succeed. Therefore, which dominoes you decide to topple, and in which direction you make them fall, will largely depend on your motivation, behavior and goals.

In a typical organization chart, the CEO or President sits at the top - the lead domino. They have the ability to influence the entire organization. The further down the chart you move, the more the positional power decreases. But even if you are the last tile in the line, you can still flex your personal power by using policies, procedures, and by reminding people of the Principles of Noble Intent that the organization espouses. Your personal power can be a catalyst for positive change. Do you remember playing with dominoes and having that last domino topple your whole beautifully positioned domino chain? No matter where you are you can have a substantial impact.

Never assume that because you have little positional power that you have no influence over those around you. Look at the diagram again. You can see that every position has at least one contact point, and, therefore, at least one avenue of persuasion or impact. Noble Intent is not just for leaders and managers; it is for everyone wanting to interact positively.

For instance, let's say someone in another department appears to be behaving maliciously. You most likely will have several opportunities to influence them. Often a simple reminder that their behavior gives the appearance of ignoring organizational policies and procedures is enough to pull them into line. Or you can simply appeal to the tenets of Noble Intent to recalibrate the person.

But the key to developing the greatest influence over the other "dominoes," is to not only know your position in the chain, but the position of everyone else. Then, once you know your position, take a long look at how you can exert the maximum impact by bringing other dominoes in line with yours. By knowing how the dominoes are laid out, you can analyze your potential impact and the impact others may have on the organization. That bit of information will help you decide with whom to align yourself and how to act in situations that can potentially affect your current position or goals. By using policies, procedures and by reminding people of the Principles of Noble Intent that the organization espouses, your personal power can be leveraged to be a catalyst for positive change.

As your reputation as a Nobler grows, so too does your ability to influence others. Therefore, fiercely guard your reputation and choose your allies wisely. Once you adopt Noble Intent as your value system, you must consistently live its tenets. It is a worthy and virtuous cause and will make you a better person.

"Do all the good you can,

By all the means you can,

In all the ways you can,

To all the souls you can,

In all the places you can,

At all the times you can,

With all the zeal you can,

As long as you ever can."

-John Wesley: John Wesley's Rule

Dedications
and Thanks

I am extremely grateful to my children, Melissa, Matthew and Alex, for teaching me about the things that are most important in life.

- Fran Landolf

As I began this project with Fran, I started to question where Noble Intent comes from. The questions that I kept asking myself: Are people born with the foundations of Noble Intent at the core of their being? Or is Noble Intent something you learn from modeling others? It is because of these questions that I think this book is so important. I believe that we are a combination of nurture and nature. We all have nurtured dispositional traits and behavioral tendencies we pick up from family, friends and what we see and hear in the media; and natural leanings that we are born with – our hardwiring. That being said, I have a few people I want to mention and thank from my nature and nurture sides.

From my nature side, I have to dedicate this book to my father, Richard (Dick) Cowie who taught me to never give up and who consistently told me that I can do anything and be anybody I want to be – I just have to work hard and be smart and keep on the right path. Good things happen to good people. My mother, Faith, succumbed to breast cancer at 40. My mother taught me that life is not always fair. But you do what you can with the hand that you are dealt and when life isn't fair, you keep your head high and you move through with grace, humor, and fortitude. I remember laughing and crying as I cut off the remnants of her hair, her joking all the while to make the task go easier on both of us. It is noble to lighten the burdens of life. Also in my gene pool is my sister, Jackie Hewitt. We are very different and very similar. Jackie is fiercely loyal, loving, funny and kind. Most important, people can depend on Jackie to be there for them, whenever needed.

From the nurture side, I have had the good fortune to meet many wonderful people and, unfortunately, I can only mention a few here. I always considered myself a spiritual person, but, later in life, as I watched my stepmother, Teresa, deal with several major tragedies in her life, I truly learned how important faith is because it sustains you and provides direction. My husband, Jack, always inspires Noble Intent in my choices. He is a giving, loving person – loyal, tried, and true – my biggest cheerleader and sounding board. I always tell people I like him better today than when we first married – and I loved him deeply then! Jazmin and Justin, my two kids, are my Noble Intent compasses. I try to lead by example and to instill in them the Principles of Noble Intent that their father and I hold dear. So far, it seems to be working. They are both fine upstanding individuals.

We interviewed a lot of people for this book and I thank them all for their time and ideas. Two people went above and beyond with their participation and comments. Editing a book is not fun – it is hard work. Gerrie Schinski and Sherry McKoy were the best type of editors we could have hoped for. Both are strong, smart women who live lives filled with Noble Intent. As such, they were insightful and terrific at asking pointed questions, proof-reading, and making wise thought-provoking comments.

My final thank you is to Lauren Hildebrand. There is always one person who steers the ship with any project and for Noble Intent it is Lauren. Fran and I talk about how much you have grown and look forward to seeing what life has to offer you. You have a fabulous future and it has been a pleasure working with you on this book.

- Hellen Davis

Chapter 1

Our Policy: Noble Intent

It's not really a policy. It's how we do business.

When Jim Schinski took over his company's Information Technology department, it had a less than desirable reputation. Other departments dreaded interacting with the tech team. It was the 'un' department - untrustworthy, uncooperative, uncommunicative and unreliable. If that wasn't enough, it was also the schoolyard bully, claiming all the company's resources for itself.

Determined to change the way his IT department did business, Schinski laid down the law. On his watch, IT would willingly cooperate and communicate with colleagues from other departments. Its members would arrive on time and contribute to meetings. Additionally, it would stop dominating all the company's assets. Doing business the "un" way would no longer be tolerated. In fact, the only "un" coming from IT would be undoing years of damage to relationships throughout the company.

Schinski introduced the IT team members to the concept of Noble Intent, a personal and professional value system based on the belief that people will live up to and often exceed expectations. The key to managing and leading with Noble Intent is to define how you will act and how you expect others to act within the context of your relationships. In business, an employee acting with Noble Intent approaches their job and colleagues in a positive, trusting manner. They unfailingly act with the best of intentions and work in the company's overall interest. They assume that every person they deal with is also acting with Noble Intent - even if they are not. They give people the benefit of the doubt. They believe that people make decisions and act because they want to make things better.

It took Schinski almost a year to get everyone on the Noble Intent bus. He drove the concepts and behaviors forward by hiring people who understood the concept readily, educating people about the tenets of Noble Intent, and by monitoring their actions and behaviors. Unfortunately, there were some staff members who refused to get on the bus to change and they were replaced, but only after giving them ample encouragement and feedback about their impact on others and providing them the opportunity to change their outlook and behaviors.

It took time and fortunately attitudes eventually changed. Once the negative influences were removed, the Noble Intent concept caught on even more quickly.

Today, Schinski's department receives the highest evaluations in the company. The turnaround hasn't gone unnoticed. The Board of Directors and the CEO went on the record saying that their Chief Information Officer is the executive they can least afford to lose. Schinski's team wholeheartedly agrees.

"Quality is never an accident; it is always the result of high intention, sincere effort, intelligent direction and skillful execution; it represents the wise choice of many alternatives."

-William A. Foster

Chapter 2

Act With and Assume Noble Intent

As we mentioned, there are two distinct facets of Noble Intent - acting and assuming. The difference is important to understand.

Acting with Noble Intent, we have found, is relatively effortless when compared to assuming Noble Intent. Why? It's all about control and choices. We each have an unchallenged command of our thoughts, words and actions; whether or not you exercise that command is another matter. Yet, once we decide that we are going to act with Noble Intent, there is nothing to stop us.

"Every great man of business has got somewhere a touch of the idealist in him."

-Woodrow Wilson

Build your foundation with Noble Intent!

Acting with Noble Intent has its benefits. For instance, our clients know that we act in business using the Principles of Noble Intent. Consequently, they assume that whatever we say or do is aimed at improving the company and its employees. In turn, we assume that when anyone of us walks into the office our personal agenda takes a backseat to our client's needs. Acting with Noble Intent is about doing the right thing; even if at times it may cost our firm business. Often, our clients would rather we tell them what they want to hear, not what they need to hear.

"Treat people as if they were what they should be, and you help them become what they are capable of becoming."

-Johann Von Goethe

If we are careful and surround ourselves with good people and select clients who share our values and goals, our agenda will align with theirs and we all win. It makes sense that if your client's values align with yours, it will lead to a greater degree of openness, and rapport will be high. When clients trust us, it gives us more freedom to say and do things others cannot. That faith allows our clients to be open to our influence and suggestions. In this way, we make a difference in our clients' organizations.

Any employee acting with Noble Intent can reap similar rewards. If your peers view you as fair and as someone who works for the common good, they will place their confidence, respect, and trust in you - even if you lack positional power. Unfortunately, the benefits and rewards don't always go to those who act with Noble Intent. We can cite many cases where the undeserving employee, misguided peer, or political player got the big office, the bonus, the budget, the recognition, or the promotion. Have faith! More often than not, those people tend to reveal themselves for what they are and alienate people at every level.

The bottom line: Even if you act with Noble Intent and assume Noble Intent, you are not always surrounded by like-minded people. But even if faced with the fact that you will sometimes find yourself dealing with people not acting with Noble Intent, you should never check your values at the door. Work through the process of understanding where the other person is coming from and attempt to influence them to do what the Principles of Noble Intent tell you is right. You can have a positive effect in a negative situation.

So, it boils down to this: What kind of person are you? And what kind of person do you aspire to be? It's your choice.

Examples of how acting with Noble Intent pays dividends for businesses are abundant. In fact, the aspect of acting with Noble Intent is one of the cornerstones of much of modern American economic theory. For example, higher wages, savings programs and health benefits for workers often leads to more production from them, benefiting not only the business owners, but the employee population.

Take Warren Buffet. In the era of corporate raiders buying and cannibalizing companies for profit, most people would agree that Buffet always acts with Noble Intent. He purchased businesses as long term investments, often improving conditions for everyone associated with the company. Most important, Buffet showed the corporate world that his philosophy isn't just good and right. He showed them that it works: for the bottom line, for the company, its employees, and shareholders.

Acting with Noble Intent works just as well in public sector organizations. General Alexander's leadership at the National Security Agency is focused on transparency in business processes and relationships. He said, "Our organization is fortunate in that we have a sense of a shared background. Noble Intent means that people have to live up to the oath and promises they make. Our oath is something we take very seriously. Every member of our organization personally swears to uphold that oath when they are hired." After stating this, General Alexander added, "The people in our organization are absolutely committed to the greater good. Noble Intent is an ongoing process, the way to create a Noble Intent culture is to follow an approach of transparency among senior leadership. That means listening respectfully to people who do not necessarily agree with you. Making sure that transparency exists ultimately lifts the clouds of suspicion."

At an offsite with his Senior leadership, General Alexander focused on decision making and how decisions are perceived. He believes that transparency is necessary for leadership support. Transparency in decision making equates to allowing all sides of an issue to be heard and to ensure that all the stakeholders in the decision understand the rationale and its underpinning. Transparency is the means of motivating people to get them to where you need them to be.

General Alexander used the awards process as an example. He said,

"I never want to hear people say, 'How did that happen?' Normally, if there are 100 facts, individuals may be cognizant of only a small subset of them." Transparency requires that you share what you know so the right decision will be made. And after the decision is made, you need to be honest and candid with your workforce. As leaders, we should be able to publicly provide the rationale for decisions. Transparency also reduces the element of surprise. If you get the reward it should be no surprise, and it should be no surprise if you didn't. Making transparent the rationale for a decision is necessary to get the support necessary for its successful implementation. People need to understand action and the consequences of inaction."

"People who act for the right reasons should be rewarded. People do observe when intent is not noble. When people are acting with Noble Intent, it always comes out."

That said, acting with and assuming Noble Intent does not require you to be naïve. If anything, Noble Intent is about giving you power to reach your goals while helping others achieve theirs with your eyes wide open to the fact that not everyone will act with nor assume Noble Intent. This book will reveal the many ways Noble Intent can help you precisely define how you and your team's actions can be ruled by Noble Intent. It will also give you what you need to assume others are acting with Noble Intent.

> If you assume Noble Intent in others, they will often match and exceed your expectations. This is a fundamental tenet of assuming Noble Intent. Conversely, if you believe people are not acting with Noble Intent, chances are they will live down to your expectations.

Remember the famous computer axiom, "garbage in, garbage out?" It means that faulty data entering a process will yield faulty output. The same holds true with people. If the person across the table believes you have decided they are unscrupulous, they have a free pass to stoop to that level and lower. They are living down to your expectations. Simply by failing to assume Noble Intent, you may have forfeited the opportunity to work constructively with that person.

Assuming Noble Intent is the knottier part of the principle. When we assume Noble Intent we must consciously trust - regardless of the signals being sent - that the people we are dealing with believe in, and are motivated by, some kind of Noble Intent. We must assume they will behave with good intentions and do the right thing based on the common good. We need to understand their position, their view of Noble Intent, and their circumstances. Even if we disagree, we must unearth their motivation so we can understand the basis of their Noble Intent.

We may have to suspend our natural instincts, beliefs and our better judgment to give the benefit of the doubt about their intentions. If after careful evaluation we conclude that our counterpart is unencumbered by the Principles of Noble Intent, we must help them correct their behavior in a non-patronizing manner. For example, they may value short-term over long-term goals or favor their personal agenda over the organization's greater good. We will explain how to tactfully help others change their behavior and have them adopt a long-term Noble Intent philosophy in a later chapter.

Some successful people think adopting Noble Intent is a crazy way to do business. They ask us why they should change and assume Noble Intent if they are already successful and have not been doing it. Our answer is simple: We want to be proud of our legacies. We want people to remember us as honest, fair and trustworthy; as people who earned our success and accomplishments without leaving footprints on others' backs along the way. And inasmuch as our success depends on others trusting us, we cannot expect to earn trust if we do not give trust. Giving trust is the most important ingredient in assuming Noble Intent. You can be successful conducting business the "old fashioned" way. Many people do so every day. We cannot deny the possibility of becoming wildly successful by not assuming Noble Intent. This would be folly. We believe, however, that even greater success is in store for those that choose to embrace Noble Intent.

> **What it really comes down to is:**
> **Who are you? What do you stand for?**
> **Are you trusted by and do you trust others?**

If you choose to act with and assume Noble Intent, you will inevitably find yourself at odds with what personal experience has taught you to be the most beneficial way to respond in certain situations. Let's say, for instance, that you discover that a colleague is trying to undermine your project. Experience directs you to DEFCON One- protect yourself and prepare to retaliate. It's almost unimaginable that you would want to take the time and make the effort to look for the person's Noble Intent when he just tossed a grenade in your direction. Furthermore, what do you do if it is the person's consistent behavior? Our experience, and that of many others, shows that assuming Noble Intent will make it easier to act with Noble Intent, and the combination nearly always achieves the desired result. No matter what they do, don't mimic their behavior. You will lose much more than you will gain.

Practicing Noble Intent does not make you the sucker that P.T. Barnum so famously said is born every minute. Noble Intent does not require you to shed decades of hard-won experience. Nor do you have to repeatedly turn the other cheek; far from it! What Noble Intent does ask is that you provide the other person the opportunity to change their behavior. Demonstrate Noble Intent through your actions of honesty, integrity, openness, and above all, treat others with dignity and respect.

> "Idealism increases in direct proportion to one's distance from the problem."
>
> -John Galsworthy

Janet found herself in a situation where her colleague was clearly not acting with Noble Intent. Janet knew that one of her peers, Sam, disliked her, though she never knew the cause of the rift. Things only got worse when an internal reorganization gave Janet direct control over Sam's group.

It wasn't long before Sam, who had gained a reputation for unprincipled behavior, began undermining Janet's authority. Through an e-mail, Sam told a lower-level employee that Janet did not like the new technology being worked by the employee. Shortly thereafter, Janet and the employee had a conversation. At the end of the conversation, the techie asked Janet why she did not like the new technology. Puzzled, Janet asked why he thought that. The employee showed Janet the e-mail. Luckily, Janet hid her emotions well.

Though Janet was furious, she realized that calling Sam into her office to express her outrage would only exacerbate their already strained relationship. Instead, she decided to find Sam's Noble Intent. There was some history to consider. For starters, she had witnessed first hand how Sam's former boss, her predecessor, had consistently undermined the work of Sam's department in meetings. Sam's former boss, no expert in the field, consistently made decisions that hurt the group without consulting Sam or the other highly qualified people on the team. In retrospect, she could see why Sam built a protective wall around his department. His team became less willing to provide information, make suggestions and offer solutions to other managers. Sam's defensive, negative behavior was why Janet, and not Sam, was named head of the division.

Janet began to wonder if Sam's behavior was actually Noble Intent distorted. Perhaps it was a pre-emptive strike protecting his team. Plausibly Sam's e-mail was a defense mechanism, an attempt to preserve what was left of his department's integrity. Understanding his motivation, Janet realized that Sam was acting within his own context of Noble Intent by trying to protect his department from a perceived threat. He was perhaps too close to the issues of his staff to look outside of his realm to see the enterprise-wide, mission consequences of his behavior.

After considering this new way of looking at Sam's behavior, Janet telephoned him and told him she wanted to correct any inaccurate information Sam might have been given. Without accusing him of anything, Janet made it clear that she actually quite liked the new technology. As a leader, she welcomed his input on important technology issues facing the company and its employees. Janet conveyed that people looked to Sam for professional guidance and that she also valued his technical expertise. With this in mind, she told him that she had just informed the management team that all technology-based decisions could not be made in the future without a comprehensive analysis from Sam and his department. She then gave him the authority to notify her if this new policy became compromised in any way and asked his advice regarding how to enforce it. Finally, she reiterated her excitement about the new technology and asked him to pass her thoughts along to anybody whom he thought had an interest.

Throughout the call, Janet never let her voice reveal negative emotions, which completely disarmed Sam, who was probably ready for a battle. Janet never mentioned the e-mail, leaving Sam to wonder if she knew about it. Confronting him about it would have been a waste of energy. She still disagreed with his actions that led up to the discussion, but Noble Intent helped her win him over. Through Noble Intent, she knew that Sam was motivated by being a strong performer. She just needed him to understand that she was there for the good of the company.

"Your greatness is measured by your kindness -

Your education and intellect by your modesty -

Your ignorance is betrayed by your suspicions and prejudices --

Your real caliber is measured by the tolerance you have for others."

-William J. Boetcker

By assuming that Sam was acting with Noble Intent from his perspective by protecting his department, Janet not only defused a confrontation, but helped a colleague change. How do WE know? Sam became a productive partner for Janet and, to our knowledge, Sam never spread another false rumor about her or her department.

Build your foundation on Noble Intent

Acting with Noble Intent doesn't just happen to the organizations any more than it will just happen to yours. Remember: There is no magic wand you can wave to make people automatically adopt the principles or act with Noble Intent. Ideally, someone in your company with a position of power - a board member, the CEO, or group leader - would first adopt Noble Intent. Then, that leader would be in a position to influence the crafting of a set of corporate values or the vision and mission statements reflecting the doctrines of Noble Intent. Empirical evidence shows that corporate declarations based on Noble Intent are not enough to generate the necessary culture change. They should be combined with leaders who also walk the walk - not just talk the talk. Declarations created by leaders who live their lives with Noble Intent and display the standards and behaviors reflected in these principles have the best shot of incorporating Noble Intent into the enterprise's business practices.

Tse-kung asked, "Is there one word that can serve as a principle of conduct for life?"

Confucius replied, "It is the word 'shu' - reciprocity."

Chapter 3

Judging the Nobility of Intentions

The more trust you earn, the more you're able to loan!
Assuming Noble Intent is granting a loan, a trust loan.

You may be wondering how the nobility of intentions is determined. Does one get to decide what does or doesn't constitute Noble Intent? Is there a grand arbitrator of all things "Noble Intent?" A judge who deems an action noble or ignoble? If so, what is one's Noble Intent touchstone? What is the acceptable moral imperative?

The answer is: "Yes, there is a grand arbitrator of Noble Intent." But it is not one person. Noble Intent is not a freewheeling, subjective experience open to individual interpretation. The adjudicator of Noble

Intent is all of us, or more precisely, society. Mankind's quest to understand right from wrong, justice from injustice, and the ethical from unethical is never-ending. Beginning with the great religious books and philosophical writings and debates, human beings have wrestled with, fought over and eventually settled upon acceptable societal standards. Those standards are constantly being refined and defined.

From the Dark Ages through the Renaissance to the current era, we have continued to evolve and add to our knowledge and intellectual growth. Throughout history we see how one great document builds upon another. In their laws and documents, sage thinkers, talented theorists, skilled physicians, visionary scientists, bold political leaders, icons of industry and brilliant academicians, took what worked and honed it. The progression from the Magna Carta (1215), detailing concessions granted from a brutal King, to the Declaration of Arbroath (1320) which set the will and wishes of the people above that of the King and affirmed Scotland's independence, set the stage for later doctrines. Many believe that the framers of the Declaration of Independence and the Constitution of the United States were inspired by those earlier works.

Mankind has pushed forward on every conceivable plane. Now, more than ever before, we are being compelled to consider how we treat each other universally with Noble Intent. The first step in that important journey came during the early part of the 20th century with the formation of the League of Nations. Today the global discussion and debate continues with the United Nations.

In that sense, then, Noble Intent is a slowly, continuously evolving concept. It is governed more by societal norms than personal interpretation, no matter how sincere the individual. Still the great thinkers of any time are instrumental in influencing the Noble Intent process and set the tone for debate. If anything is clear, it is that Noble Intent is not a cafeteria of values from which one may pick and choose. Ruthless dictators or blood thirsty terrorists don't operate under the Principles of Noble Intent. Why? Because their actions and intentions go against society's norms. Noble Intent is a relational, active concept between people. But even more important, Noble Intent expects adherence to society's accepted standards - not an individual's interpretation - of what is right, just and ethical.

But how do we know if an intention is really noble and good? An intention is just that, until acted upon. If we do believe that most people act with Noble Intent, then we must assume Noble Intent in others. Yet, how do we determine the person's intention? Deciding this question is precisely why every legal system has varying degrees of sentences. The judge or jury must determine whether or not the person was acting with malicious intent. They do so after careful consideration of the evidence. Sentences are usually more severe if premeditated malicious intent is found and less punitive if not. In the legal system, self defense, manslaughter, murder in the second degree or first degree all bring different sentences. In the United States, we assume innocence until proven guilty. This is society's way of institutionalizing the assumption of Noble Intent. We give the accused the benefit of the doubt, even if it appears that little doubt exists.

We have determined that actions that result in the same effect have different classifications according to motivation and circumstances. It is safe to say that most people agree that it is generally wrong to hurt others. But there are exceptions to the rule, such as self-defense or when helping or saving someone's life. In each case, you may have to inflict a degree of pain on another human being. But in each case, it is not only socially acceptable, but absolutely necessary. The circumstance and context transforms a seemingly bad action into a good one.

Now, let's imagine that your attempt to save a person goes wrong. The result is that the person is paralyzed or, worse, dies. Doctors, firemen, police and rescue workers face this everyday. The rescuer's actions are socially acceptable because their intentions were authentic. Indeed, if you genuinely mean well, you act with Noble Intent. Helping people is acting with Noble Intent.

In the corporate world, feedback, a warning, sanctions, losing a professional license and termination are all examples of inflicting acceptable and necessary pain. All must be judged by the corporate body, according to the perpetrator's intention. These judgments should be fair and able to stand the test of time.

Ideally, Noble Intent should not be situational. Of course, at one time or another, we have all fooled ourselves and others with selfish acts duplicitously masquerading as altruistic and pure.

"A man's true greatness lies in the consciousness of an honest purpose in life, founded on a just estimate of himself and everything else, on frequent self-examinations, and a steady obedience to the rule which he knows to be right."

-Marcus Aurelius Antoninus

The real test to find out if our intention is noble and good in the face of an ethical dilemma, is to try to generalize and universalize the action so that it works in all situations. Just taking the time to consider whether this is in accordance with Principles of Noble Intent will prove valuable. Weigh the evidence and make your Noble Intent judgment based on societal norms.

Situational Ethics 101

Context and circumstance, however, do not justify bad actions. For example, have you ever found yourself in a situation where you know what you are about to do is wrong, but you try justifying it by thinking, "If people knew what I knew, and had to go through what I am going through, they would understand and surely condone what I am about to do." Welcome to Situational Ethics 101. You are adjusting your beliefs and behavior to fit the circumstances to legitimatize your action. In short, you are creating an excuse for doing something you know is wrong. But your excuse does not transform the situation.

What about truly evil people? We advocate assuming Noble Intent, even if we do not necessarily agree with someone's actions or the consequences. For example, Mohammad Hejazi, commander of an Iranian paramilitary unit, claims that "the suicide bomber's goals might be noble, but their means are not correct1." He assumes Noble Intent in the suicide bomber in order to better understand the person's motivation to commit heinous acts. We and Mohammad Hejazi, of course, disagree with the bomber's methods. To seek understanding of the bomber's motivation, we assume the bomber has a warped sense of Noble Intent and thinks that they are operating with Noble Intent. This type of understanding will help us be in a better position to influence. Without understanding the other party's way of thinking, it is not easy to be effective in trying to argue or fight for peaceful methods. The bomber thinks that the world will be somehow made better by murdering people who do not agree with his religious beliefs.

By making an effort to understand someone's intentions, you place their individual motivations and actions within the greater socio-cultural context. When we make an effort to understand why people do what they do, we can better communicate with them. If someone feels understood, they are more likely to listen and, in the case of people acting ignobly as in the case of the bomber, such an understanding can only add a persuasively powerful advantage when seeking out an argument to change their reprehensible methods.

---

1 Shargh, July 22, 2006

Chapter 4

The Butterfly Effect & The Domino Effect

In 1960, Massachusetts Institute of Technology ("MIT") meteorologist Edward Lorenz set up a computer program to study a weather prediction problem. According to Chaos Theory: A Brief Introduction, MIT's Lorenz didn't set out to accurately predict weather. Rather, he wanted to predict what the weather might produce. His goal was to attempt to find the underlying order in apparently random data. Thus, was born the "Chaos Theory."

Fortunately, the story doesn't end there. Using his computer, he created simple graphs of data gleaned from thousands of pages of printed data. He noticed that very slight changes in one variable had profound effects on the behavior of the graphs that depended on that variable. So if one graph represented a solution for a given set of initial conditions (perhaps a weather prediction from a given point in time), then changing the set of initial conditions even slightly led to a radically different graph (a very different weather prediction from the same point in time). This became known as the "Butterfly Effect."

Building on Lorenz's Butterfly Effect Theory, Ian Stewart in his book, Does God Play Dice? The Mathematics of Chaos explains that the single flap of a butterfly's wings produces tiny changes in the atmosphere that, over time, may have unimaginable repercussions. In essence, he discovered that minute changes today may have enormous effects over time.

"So, in a month's time, a typhoon that would have devastated the Indonesian coast doesn't happen," he writes. "Or maybe one that wasn't going to occur, does." Interesting? Certainly. Yet, what does a complicated mathematics and physics theory and its consequences have to do with Noble Intent? Just this - when you act with Noble Intent, your smallest, seemingly most insignificant act has the potential to make a huge difference. Over time, just like the butterfly instinctively flapping its wings in a faraway jungle, you will probably never know whose life you have impacted or how you have changed it.

Noble Intent should be selfless. You should never expect recognition or some other tangible reward for acting with, or assuming, Noble Intent. By living with Noble Intent daily, you will benefit from the internal serenity that is derived from a life well lived. Noble Intent is, by definition, a completely selfless concept.

There are scores of well-known people for whom Noble Intent is at least, in part, responsible for their fame. Although, there are scores more who never receive or expect credit for their Noble Intent. You may have heard of Alex from the Alex's Lemonade Stands that have cropped up like dandelions across the country during the past few years. Two days before her first birthday in 1997, a CAT scan found a tumor on Alex's spine. It was neuroblastoma, a childhood cancer. Alex had the form that kills one out of three children.

Several years later while recovering in the hospital from a failed stem cell replacement procedure, Alex told her parents, Jay and Liz Scott, she wanted to have a lemonade stand that summer. She wanted to give all the proceeds to the hospital to help kids with cancer. Her parents thought it was a cute idea yet concluded that with all Alex was going through, she would probably forget her goal. They could not have been more wrong! That summer Alex started nagging. They probably thought that her big goal of giving the money to charity was not worth it for their sick daughter to sit outside in the hot sun selling lemonade only to raise a few dollars. Jay thought his daughter might collect $20 and the risk to her health was not worth the reward. Fortunately, Alex continued pleading and by July her parents gave in.

The day of the sale Alex was up at 5:30 a.m., dressed and ready to go. To everyone's amazement, the tenacious Alex sat at the stand all day. People came and kept on coming and at the end of the day Alex sold more than $2,000 worth of

"Not being always able to follow others exactly, nor attain to the excellence of those he imitates, a prudent man should always follow the path trodden by great men and imitate those who are most excellent, so that if he does not attain their greatness, at any rate he will get some tinge of it.."

-Niccolo Di Bernardo

lemonade. Every ensuing year the lemonade stand grew until they had sprouted up all over America, Canada, Europe and Japan. Remarkably, each year the profits grew, surpassing $1 million in 2004.

Sadly, Alex succumbed to the cancer on August 1, 2004. In an interview with People magazine the year before she died, Alex said she liked raising the money because she knew the doctors needed it to help other people. In June 2006, Alex's Lemonade Stands Foundation announced it had raised more than $6 million for childhood cancer research. "Everyone says she is an inspiration to them and that she has touched their lives," Liz Scott told People. "They come from all ages, all walks of life and all backgrounds."

There is no doubt that Alex was a very special child. Fortunately, there are regular work-a-day people who live their lives and do their jobs with Noble Intent. Teachers, quickly come to mind. They rarely, if ever, know what life-changing effect they have had on their students. If you think about it for a moment, teachers have a profound impact on our lives. They are the people who pour the foundations of basic math, science, grammar and reading upon which we build our futures. If you cannot add, subtract or read it is exceedingly difficult to become a productive citizen in the real world. If you can do your multiplication tables from memory or love reading, it is probably due to a dedicated teacher.

Yet, most of us have never called or written our teachers - or for that matter any instructor or professor - to say thanks. Nor have we recognized their contributions to any of our successes in life. We venture to guess that most of us probably never will.

Nevertheless, every day teachers across the country go into their classrooms and start drilling those same fundamentals to the next generation of students. They seem unfazed by our lack of acknowledgement. It does not lessen the importance of their work. They intrinsically understand - which is probably why they are called to the teaching profession - that what they are doing is somehow connected to a larger universe, a higher power. Receiving recognition is not their motivation. They know that it often takes a thousand little things to create one very big, important accomplishment. The work is their reward and perhaps the understanding and faith in knowing that they do make a difference in so many young lives is precisely how they sustain their motivation.

Now, let's move from the classroom to the meeting room. You have decided to adopt Noble Intent as a lifestyle and to practice it every day. At today's meeting you act, as always, with Noble Intent. By doing so, you might have unknowingly influenced other people at the meeting to act differently than they planned. For instance, you were not aware that members of another department had planned to undercut your proposal. But by acting with Noble Intent, you changed their minds. Why? From the way you treated them and communicated with them from a solid standing in Noble Intent, they might have listened with respect to your ideas.

You put reciprocity into play. By acting with Noble Intent towards them, they reciprocate in turn by treating you better. By listening to you as you listened to them, they become open and now understand that your plan took into consideration the greater good of everyone. You were not just looking out for your own department's needs after all. They recognized that you really did take into account how this decision would negatively impact their budget and resource planning. Furthermore, while you may have had an inkling that the other department planned to thwart your proposal, your words and actions showed only that you assumed they were acting only for the benefit of the business and not to protect their turf. Bottom line: By assuming and acting with Noble Intent, you communicated in a respectful way, encouraging others to do the same, resulting in everyone buying into what was best for the company.

While you may never connect the dots between your actions and the positive outcomes, have faith that over time there will be benefits to the organization. This is the Noble Intent domino effect at work.

Intentional Noble Intent

Todd Trapp practices his own brand of Noble Intent. He calls it intentional Noble Intent.

"Intentional is when you are thinking about Noble Intent and how it applies" to a situation, said Trapp, a regional engineering director for Raytheon Company, supervising 700 employees.

A born optimist, Trapp has always been a glass-half-full kind of guy who naturally sees the good in people. He never gave his approach to life and people a name until he heard about Noble Intent. It was the perfect fit.

"A man is the part he plays among his fellows. He is not isolated; he cannot be. His life is made up of the relations he bears to others - is made or marred by those relations, guided by them. There is nothing else upon which he can spend his spirit - nothing else that we can see. It is by these he gets his spiritual growth; it is by these we see his character revealed, his purpose, his gifts. A few men act as those who have mastered the secrets of a serious art, with deliberate subordination of themselves to the great end and motive of the play. These have found themselves, and have all the ease of a perfect adjustment."

-Woodrow Wilson

"Noble Intent really is how I think I live my life," he said. "In general, I find Noble Intent to meet my life philosophy. I've got a list of laws and one is: 'When in doubt, take the high road.'"

Two years ago, Raytheon asked Trapp to take another road and relocate to Florida. The company needed someone with a positive attitude to help rebuild a troubled business region. The group had suffered through several buyouts and name changes and had taken a decidedly defensive posture toward the corporation. "There were serious issues of self-confidence and organization confidence," Trapp said. "Leadership did not support the corporation and that fed a mindset of us versus them."

As Trapp drove into work that first morning, he realized he did not know anyone at the site, including his secretary. "I thought, oh my God, you are stupid,'" he said to himself.

Trapp acknowledged that the job had, at times, challenged his optimism and Noble Intent. He still did not understand why his colleagues and subordinates were reluctant to trust him or believe that what he was doing was in everyone's best interest.

"There is nothing more painful than when you do something with the best of intention and people read it as you are doing it for personal gain," he said. "That can be a detractor to acting with Noble Intent to some extent. That is my challenge. How do you drive Noble Intent through in a culture of 700 people that started in a very dark place a few years ago?"

One way is to communicate, communicate, communicate. Trapp rediscovered the value of open dialogue recently when a group under his supervision started a project. Instead of just buying material from a subcontractor, like it normally did, the group needed a more involved, ongoing relationship with the vendor. Four vice presidents signed on as project sponsors. No one, however, told the head of the supply chain about the unique circumstances. Consequently, the supply chain manager thought that Trapp was undermining his position. So, the supply chain manager counterattacked by floating a few rumors. That was enough to bring a visit by Trapp to set the record straight and apologize.

"I realized what it must have looked like to him and I understood that the guy was protecting his organization," Trapp said. "But he was putting things on me that were not true." The supply chain manager was definitely not assuming Noble Intent!

Trapp explained the project and the two reached an understanding. "We got past that and now we are co-advocates of the position," Trapp said. Getting people to believe in and practice Noble Intent with every action will not be easy. But Trapp is determined. His plan calls for first converting his team and front line leaders and then letting them spread the word.

"I believe that people in (leadership) positions, by and large, are acting with Noble Intent," he said. "Sometimes people may act with misplaced Noble Intent. In a lot of cases they are working from a position of fear."

That is where intentional Noble Intent comes into play. Trapp wants to set things up so that employees see management following through on acting and assuming Noble Intent. Even more important, he wants his team and the front line leaders to be on the lookout for people doing the right thing so they can be rewarded.

"When you catch people doing good, you reinforce it," he said. "You can be intentional. As I want to accelerate the Noble Intent culture, we can look for opportunities to reinforce it. You have to give people the opportunity to build trust. You just have to keep at it. No one word will change people's mindset. It's all about being consistent and intentional."

Another area where Noble Intent can play a role is during coaching sessions and while giving feedback. After all, who can argue with the guidance and feedback you receive when it is dispensed with Noble Intent - that is in the best interest of the person and company.

"Noble Intent plays a powerful role in giving constructive feedback to people," Trapp said. Even for a glass-half-full guy, taking over a division so awash in negativity had to be daunting. At the very least, Trapp's stress levels had to have gone through the roof. Not really. "I have less stress than almost everyone in the organization," he said. "As long as you are acting with Noble Intent, what is the worse thing that can happen?"

Chapter 5

The Benefits of Acting with Noble Intent

WOW! I would have never expected that adopting a culture of Noble Intent would have such a dramatic impact on our bottom line.

No·bler: \nō-blər\ One who acts with and assumes Noble Intent

Every year, American businesses lose millions of dollars to stress-related claims. The Centers for Disease Control and Prevention and the National Institute for Occupational Safety and Health report that in the 21st century, stress will be responsible for more lost days than any other factor.

Stress Reduction

In fact, one of the most palpable benefits associated with Noble Intent is stress reduction. How specifically does Noble Intent reduce stress? The reasons are pretty clear when you consider what causes stress at work. How about adversarial relationships? Reactionary behavior? Back room politics? Back stabbing, unethical connivers? Hidden agendas? Not being trusted, just to name a few. It is clear that people who do not act with Noble Intent also do not assume Noble Intent on the part of others. It is an almost physical impossibility to assume others are honest and trustworthy if you yourself do not display these same attributes.

If we are at our best as human beings when we act with Noble Intent, won't that automatically reduce stress? These stressors do not immediately disappear, but people can erode their effects over time. This takes time. By consistently striving towards Noble Intent, negative behavior, actions, and conspiracies begin to lose effect. People will feel stress reduction because the negative effects of unacceptable behavior, damaging actions and business-killing conspiracies will diminish.

Consequences of Not Acting with Noble Intent

Removing a manager from the responsibility chain is never Jim Torgerson's first option. But he says that a CEO does not have the luxury of allowing one individual to undermine a decision made in the best interest of the client, the company, and the employees.

"People will work at cross purposes to what you want to accomplish either because they think they know better or they have their own agenda," Torgerson said. "You have to confront them once you recognize what is going on. You have to either get them in line or take them out of line. Usually if you point out what impact they are having, and why this is not acceptable, they usually get in line."

For whatever reason, people do not always fall in line. That is when the CEO has to be resolute. At one company, Torgerson had to reign in the Chief Financial Officer ("CFO"), who was also head of Human Resources ("HR"). Along with people complaining that the man was verbally abusive, he seemed to be working his own agenda.

"You just have to take those people on and make sure they understand what is acceptable and what isn't," Torgerson said. "If people are out for themselves, they are not going to be on my team!"

Torgerson firmly laid down the law with the CFO. He explained what he said when he confronted his executive. Torgerson told him, "This behavior does not work. I place a high value on employees and their morale." For a while, the CFO seemed to get better but ultimately Torgerson decided the CFO was ill-suited to be responsible for HR. He was a smart financial person, but he didn't have the personality, employee confidence, or employee trust to lead people in that department.

Talking doesn't always work but clearly explaining your goals and metrics for success are usually effective in turning the person around. You must explain the consequences of their behavior. You can't have one person destroy a team or hurt employees and their morale. Torgerson ultimately had to let the CFO know who was in charge by taking away his HR management responsibilities because his attempt to deal with him nobly did not work. In making the change, the greater good was served.

Acting nobly for the benefit of the employees sometimes has negative consequences for the leader. "I don't think I'm mean, but the facts are what they are, and you just have to deal with it," Torgerson said. "Some people can't manage and can't direct people well. They don't always have the right skill sets, but often they are very smart and have a particular talent you need. So acting nobly is when a leader puts them in a role for success and where they don't influence others negatively. You just cannot allow them to cause undue stress to others and the business at large."

Instead of firing an employee, Torgerson would rather work with people to help them keep their job. Over the years, he has saved many employees targeted for termination by the board. His willingness to work with people who want to grow and improve professionally really is what Noble Intent is about -- helping people.

"I really do believe that the vast majority of people - probably just about everybody - want to do the right thing," he said. "My assumption is that people want to do the right thing and have Noble Intent. That is the premise that I start with and we go from there."

Consistency is the Key

Most important, if individuals consistently act with and assume Noble Intent, they will respect themselves. It is reassuring and much healthier to no longer wake up in the middle of the night worrying about whether you have done the right thing or whether you have said the right thing. Acting with Noble Intent is about ALWAYS doing the right thing. Acting with Noble Intent not only helps you, it helps those around you. Stress around the office is lowered because people know what to consistently expect from others. They know that people will treat them with courtesy and respect even when they bring bad news.

Attitude

Just imagine you have a bad day. No one said Noble Intent inoculated you from being human! If your organization's people practice Noble Intent, people are more willing to "cut you some slack." They see a bad day as an anomaly rather than the general rule of your behavior. Therefore, they trust that you will return to your normal Noble Intent behavior patterns. They realize that you are human and they understand that what goes around comes around. If they react negatively to your negativity, it probably won't make you more positive!

Another benefit is that it is difficult to remain in a bad mood. If you act with Noble Intent you recognize quickly that the world does not revolve around you. It's about making sure everyone around you have what they need for success. It is tough to stay in a bad mood if you are cheering on others.

Hellen's friend Pat Croce, the former president of the Philadelphia 76ers and nationally known motivational speaker, is unarguably one of the most upbeat, positive people on the planet. Pat lives a life of Noble Intent. Ask him how he feels and he'll tell you that he feels great. He honestly means it and lives it on a daily basis. Even when he is not having the best day, Pat still feels good because he understands that it isn't all about him. He understands that Noble Intent means getting out of the "me" mode to see what you can do for someone else.

A native Philadelphian, Pat desperately wanted the 76ers to bring the city a championship followed by the mandatory victory parade down Broad Street, right through the center of the city. In the event the Sixers could not do it, Pat was perfectly fine with any of the city's other professional teams - Flyers, Eagles, Phillies - celebrating a championship. He just wanted the City of Brotherly Love to feel great.

"There are three marks of a superior man: being virtuous, he is free from anxiety; being wise, he is free from perplexity; being brave, he is free from fear."

-Confucius

So how do you, like Pat, set the wheels of Noble Intent in motion and maintain momentum? Let's reiterate that the concept of Noble Intent is fairly easy to grasp, intuitive really. Yet, we must recognize implementing the philosophy is difficult and sustaining the lifestyle is even harder still. Suffice it to say that Noble Intent is not accomplished by clicking a button on your TV remote. Think of it as mastering an instrument. Even a virtuoso must practice every day to stay at their best. Fortunately, the more time and effort spent on Noble Intent, the more ingrained it becomes and the more benefits you reap.

Noble Intent Challenges You

When you begin acting with Noble Intent expect to be personally and professionally challenged. Whenever tempted to abandon Noble Intent, think carefully about your actions. Trusting people who have not earned your trust is challenging at best. However, over time it will pay dividends.

If you are in a leadership position, people should clearly understand that as the department leader you can most certainly set up behavioral norms, expectations, and parameters based on Principles of Noble Intent. Convey why it is critically important that they be consistent with the principles. Bottom line: Even if you cannot change their thinking to that of Noble Intent, you can set the parameters for their behavior and actions when they work in organizations that you lead.

The nay-sayers will obviously feel uncomfortable working in a Noble Intent environment. They will have no one to conspire with, no one to gossip with, and no one to build an alliance to undercut the direction you've set. Chances are they will try to coerce one or more of your employees. Don't let them. They are a bad influence and here are your only two choices: They must change, or ultimately they will have to go. The best-case scenario is if they decide to change on their own. Failing this, they might become so uncomfortable when they see that you are holding them accountable to the principles that they will leave on their own. In the worse-case scenario, you will have to terminate them before they undermine the greater good. That was the situation Schinski faced when he took over the IT department at his company that we discussed in the first chapter.

When everyone across the enterprise, from teams to departments to regions, is on the same page, positive morale, increased productivity and enhanced innovation and creativity will proliferate. But it won't happen with one conversation or one workshop on Noble Intent.

Noble Intent Like-Mindedness

Once Noble Intent takes root, you will begin attracting like-minded people to your organization. In fact, you may be surprised by the number of people who already act with Noble Intent at your company. You just have not recognized them. Now that you do, it may be worthwhile to set up a program that acknowledges the "Noble Intent Employee of the Month." This could be as simple as establishing a peer recognition program. Any person could nominate a person or team that best exemplifies the Principles of Noble Intent. A peer review team would meet regularly to review the nominations and weigh them according to their impact. The review team would select the best example of Noble Intent behavior having the greatest positive impact on the mission or on the company's bottom line. Public recognition of the winning nominee by leadership and ongoing tangible public and private reminders that Noble Intent is indeed something leadership values will reinforce Noble Intent behavior throughout your organization. To ensure that behavior that is noble stands out and is rewarded accordingly, building metrics around the program may be necessary to ensure its value and success.

Granting Loans and Making Trust Deposits

Assuming Noble Intent often requires us to overcome our preconceived notions and at times our best judgment regarding what exactly motivates behaviors in others. So the act of assuming Noble Intent when all evidence and intuition points otherwise requires an enormous leap of faith. An appropriate metaphor that helps explain that leap of faith is the act of lending trust or granting a "trust loan." When we assume Noble Intent we lend trust to the recipient with an expectation of a return on that trust-loan investment. That return may benefit the enterprise as a whole, and may not directly benefit us personally. Preconceived notions and judgment may dictate that assumption of Noble Intent is not warranted. You might conclude that the person is not trustworthy. Perhaps the recipient is not Noble Intent creditworthy thus not worth the risk of a trust investment. This may be a consequence of several defaults on previous trust loans, or the result of behavior so egregious as to destroy any expectation of return on the investment of a trust loan.

"A leader of men must make decisions quickly; be independent; act and stand firm; be a fighter; speak openly, plainly, frankly; make defeats his lessons; cooperate; co-ordinate; use the best of any alliances or allies; walk with active faith courageously toward danger or the unknown; create a staff; know, love and represent the best interests of his followers; be loyal, true, frank and faithful; reward loyalty, have a high intelligence and worthy purpose and ideal. Do justice; love mercy; fear no man but fear only God."

-John W. Dodge

I've earned some more trust. Put it in my account where we can collectively use it to make loans when we need to assume Noble Intent.

We asked General Alexander, Director, National Security Agency/Chief, Central Security Service (NSA/CSS), what he thought about trusting in situations where trust had not been earned - the Noble Intent concept of making a trust loan. "Lending trust equates to personal courage. I've had bosses who very vocally say that they see things very differently than me. I consider it my moral responsibility to lay out the facts as I see them. If you don't assume this responsibility, you are faced with two things. First, you lack personal courage. Second, you have lost the opportunity to have an impact by proceeding with transparency and integrity. This is something that must be learned and practiced and it must be a part of your value set."

"A character standard is far more important than ever a gold standard. The success of all economic systems is still dependent upon both righteous leaders and righteous people."

-Roger W. Babson

Trust is just as important in the private sector as the public sector. Trust is perhaps the single most important word in a financial planner's lexicon. Without the client's trust, a financial planner would be just another well-educated, snappily dressed, unemployed expert.

But trust is vital when it comes to personal finances. Clients, after all, are exposing their most personal and guarded information to someone who, in many cases, was a stranger not all that long ago. The client needs to believe that their financial planner will not only do them no harm, but is savvy enough to enhance their portfolio. But often the decision to hire a financial planner comes down to a feeling. That feeling is called trust, the bedrock of Noble Intent.

Cheryl Creuzot learned early on about the role of trust in financial planning. Understanding that importance has helped Creuzot become a successful financial planner and president of Wealth Development Strategies, L.P., a comprehensive financial planning firm.

Cruezot recognized early in her career that everyone was not good all the time or nor do they necessarily operate with Noble Intent in all situations. But even if others behaved that way it did not mean that she could not operate with Noble

Intent. She believes that she can still have a positive outcome despite another person's lack of Noble Intent. "Everything is about trust in financial planning I have gone through a number of personal and business experiences that have been negative and damaging and hurtful, but mostly you realize that it's a small number that are negative experiences," she said. "You realize that people are mostly very good. You have to live your life expecting that of people. I have a philosophy that people can only give what they have. They think and act the way they do because of their life experiences. They are the way they are for a reason.

"Noble Intent involves taking a risk," said Creuzot. "If you go out there and assume the best of people, that has some risk attached to it. You can be disappointed. It may be they are not the noble person you thought they were or expected them to be. People let you down. It's part of life so it's part of business. You can have Noble Intent but I think you can also have your eyes wide open.

"I think Noble Intent is in the realm of having a positive mindset and positive thinking," she said. "And you have to have a positive mindset to be successful at anything. I feel safer because of the life experiences that I have had and the spiritual journey that I've gone on," she said. "I do not worry about being hurt or damaged, whether business-wise or personally. I'm solid in my convictions and beliefs; and that makes me strong. So if you don't have that fear, you don't have to put on that armor. If you have that armor on, human beings can sense it. If you are open, honest, and relaxed and there to receive good and expect good, I think people feel and sense that in your intentions.

"Noble Intent comes with time," she said. "It is a choice and an experience thing. You choose to have Noble Intent. It is a journey. I definitely think it is a choice."

"You are today where your thoughts have brought you; you will be tomorrow where your thoughts take you. You cannot escape the result of your thoughts, but you can endure and learn, can accept and be glad.....
Into your hands... receive that which you earn; no more, no less."

-James Lane Allen

Chapter 6

Nature Versus Nurture - Growing Yourself

Growing people by sowing the seeds of Noble Intent.

This question is one of mankind's oldest, continuous, and unresolved debates: Which has more impact throughout a person's life, nature or nurture. Although it has been argued for thousands of years, one of the earliest recorded mentions of the phrase "nature versus nurture" as a way of discussing heredity and environment goes back to a 13th Century French play called Silence.

Eight centuries later, there has been anything but silence on the topic. Scientists agree that our eye and hair colors are inherited from genes our ancestors give us. Some scientists also believe that we are also genetically predisposed for intelligence, personality, skills, abilities, and other behaviors. So if you are shy, gregarious, musically or athletically talented, a good or bad mathematician, a risk taker or conservative, they suggest you should thank your parents and their genetic pool.

On the other hand, people who favor the nurture position do not deny that genetic tendencies exist. However, they think that how you were raised is the dominant factor in who you are. Nurture philosophy supporters just do not think that genetic predisposition matters as much as how you developed in your surroundings and were encouraged or nurtured by those closest to you. They believe that anyone raised in the right environment can learn any skill, master any talent, or become an expert in a given area of knowledge, if they have the will, the brains, and the environment.

Nurture philosophy supporters do recognize that genetics play a role in I.Q. They also contend that the influence exerted by family, religious organizations, friends, peers, role models, and mentors has more to do with the person you become. So, if you want to be a chess whiz, join a chess club. Find someone who is a chess master, learn from that person, and then play with others who are better skilled than you are so that you can pick up even more information. In this way, you become better because of a nurturing environment - even if you weren't born predestined to become a chess master by way of your gene pool.

If you are afraid to speak at business meetings, a mentor who is nurturing you might point out how important it is to overcome this issue. They might just give you the confidence you need. To overcome your fear, look at the options available in your natural environment. You could go to your local library and read about how others have overcome a similar problem, seek the help of a seasoned public speaker who lives down the street, improve your skill set by watching debates, join a Toastmasters International group or just ask to present more reports. Again, the environment you dwell in provides the knowledge and gives you the impetus to grow and change. In this regard, it doesn't really matter whether you are a naturally talented speaker or not. It would be nice, but it's not a prerequisite.

Begun formally in 1990, the U.S. Human Genome Project was a 13-year effort coordinated by the U.S. Department of Energy and the National Institutes of Health. The project's goal was to identify all the approximately 20,000-25,000 genes in human DNA and improve tools for data analysis. The U.S. Human Genome Project has given us new information about nature versus nurture. Scientists say that genes play a very important role. Scientists also say that environmental influences are also important for individual differences in those complex traits. Boil it down, and the research seems to be saying that we become who we are because of nature and nurture. For instance, you may possess the gene that gives you the hand-eye coordination to hit a baseball 400 feet. But if you are raised in an environment where baseball is not an important sport, you may not be given the opportunity to play. Consequently, you may never showcase that ability.

> The debate of nature versus nurture plays a critical role in Noble Intent. We really don't have much control over nature. That being said, as a leader you have to learn the fundamentals of how to nurture Noble Intent in your people.

Many people just seem to be born good. They were sweet babies who grew up to be kind, thoughtful children. Later they turned out to be the best boss you ever had the pleasure of working with. Noble Intent is usually learned through experience and not the result of genetic predisposition.

Let's assume that for Noble Intent you agree that nurture is more powerful than nature. If you are someone who grew up in a household that espoused principles similar to the Principles of Noble Intent, your thinking and behavior patterns are most likely the result of a nurturing Noble Intent environment. That said, there is a greater chance that you will in turn live these principles because not doing so would be contrary to the deeply held beliefs that your socialization produced. Not doing so would create a great deal of stress.

Nurturing Noble Intent

People who learn Noble Intent early in life are often unaware of how, where, or even when they were introduced to the value system. Many are well into adulthood before they realize how they received the priceless gift of an enduring moral compass.

If you are in a leadership position and you were nurtured in a Noble Intent environment, chances are you will advocate these doctrines in your corporate life. The Noble Intent ideals, doctrines, and theories that your parents and your social circle promoted are so well engrained in your psyche that, unintentionally or not, you have probably already been teaching others the same set of principles and behavioral guidelines through your words and actions - just as they taught you.

For Lieutenant General Paul E. Blackwell that moment came after buying back every acre of his grandfather's South Carolina farm. The family had been forced to sell it when the old man died in 1961. Blackwell bought it back to honor his grandfather's legacy.

"I guess there is Noble Intent in families and tradition," the General said.

A decorated and highly- respected officer, General Blackwell rose through the ranks, beginning his military career as a second lieutenant in the infantry. When he retired in 1996, the General had held no less than 12 command positions, including two tours of duty in Vietnam, and with the Third Armor Division in Desert Storm. His final military post was as Deputy Chief of Staff for Operations and Plans for the U.S. Army. He transitioned to the private sector and is currently vice president for the Rapid Initiatives Group of Network Centric Systems (NCS), Raytheon.

Throughout his career General Blackwell was introduced to a library full of leadership and motivational techniques. Yet, when it came to working with people, Blackwell found himself relying on the lessons learned at his grandfather's knee. The old man, a poor cotton and corn farmer, always trusted people and looked for the goodness in others. It was a lesson that General Blackwell took with him to every one of his commands across the world.

Like others who practice Noble Intent, Blackwell believes that people are intrinsically good and will almost certainly exceed expectations. That may sound naïve coming from a military commander who has seen the horrors of combat. But the military actually depends on its soldiers and commanders practicing Noble Intent.

"Noble Intent is a very important aspect in the military or industry," he said. "The truth is you have to put the good of the organization, the good of the entity in which you are involved, above personal goals. If you do not take a personal risk in combat to accomplish the mission, you will not achieve success and clearly you are not living up to your promise to act with Noble Intent."

For military leaders, assuming Noble Intent means training troops to the highest standard. It is a leader's duty to articulate the vision, goals, and objectives of a mission and to lead by example. Once the vision, goals and objectives are conveyed, soldiers are expected to have the confidence and trust in their leader necessary to execute the mission. The soldiers are expected to assume that their leaders are acting with Noble Intent.

"Having confidence, in my mind, is the applicable part of assuming Noble Intent," Blackwell said. "It says: I give guidance to my subordinates and allow them to succeed. It is building on a success-oriented attitude and encouraging others. I think there is almost a religious focus or aspect of Noble Intent because it is about trusting people."

While military leaders must trust their subordinates, they must still verify that things are being done properly. If not, the leader must make the necessary corrections. The difference is that a leader practicing Noble Intent will believe that the person who failed wanted to succeed and was acting with and assuming Noble Intent. For military or industry leaders, assuming Noble Intent gives a completely different slant to mentoring and tutoring.

"We have to give people freedom to succeed," Blackwell said. "We talk a lot about that but once you assume Noble Intent you will give people the freedom to succeed. Noble Intent really is about, and life is about, and success is about, having a value system that believes in people."

Today as a business leader, Blackwell has seen corporate leaders practice Noble Intent. But the number who do is far fewer than he expected. He cites Wall Street's unflinching eye on the bottom line as the reason.

"I think there is a great driving force in the corporate world to achieve numbers above all else," he said. "I guess you could say cash is very important and it is critical to make the financial goals established, no matter if you are a shoe salesman driven to sell shoes or the CEO of a company. Fear of failure, rather than acting with or assuming Noble Intent, may tend to drive people, too. This is a slippery slope that should be avoided."

Even the corporate leaders who do exhibit Noble Intent may tend to revert to their old ways when their numbers fall. While the bottom line is important, getting excellent results doesn't exclude the ethical trusted needed by achieving those results with nobility.

"It does not become second nature during periods of adversity unless Noble Intent is deeply ingrained in the way you do business," he said.

Whether in good times or bad, Blackwell's Noble Intent was always second nature. Most likely that was because it had been ingrained in him as a child listening to and watching his grandfather.

"An ideal is the only thing that has any real force. We have lost sight of our own ideal and its tremendous force and vigor. Somehow that must be recaptured. It must be passed on to generations to come, to make them believe in it, so that the energy in man which has its source in the ideal will not be lost."

-Homer Ferguson

It all started to become clear to him when he thought about why, 17 years after his grandfather died and the farm was sold, that he felt the need to buy back every acre.

"I think there clearly was, in my mind, the fact that when I looked at my grandfather, who was dirt poor, worked in a mill and farmed, that he was the epitome of goodness," he said. "I think the Noble Intent there was to continue the Noble Intent he had demonstrated in life."

General Blackwell understood that bringing the farm back into the family was his way to both thank his grandfather and honor his legacy. Beginning in 1978 and for the next 15 years, he bought back chunks of land - five acres here, 15 acres there - until in 1995 he settled on the final 25 acres. The last purchase included the old farmhouse built in 1920. Then Blackwell fulfilled his grandfather's dream by adding a pond to the property.

"He saw goodness in people and felt he was a trustworthy kind of guy," Blackwell said. "I guess I would tell you that Noble Intent is taught by family relationships that carry beyond and evolve into the world."

"Do not impose on others what you yourself do not desire."

- *Confucianism*, Doctrine of the Mean 13.3

Chapter 7

Noble Intent & Your Conscience

It is a beautiful idea that every man has within a Guardian Angel;
and that it is true, too, for Conscience is ever on the watch,
ever ready to warn us of danger.

- Anonymous

You can change the way you think, if you learn how to take control of your internal voice. Your current self-talk (your internal voice) can be exchanged, erased, replaced, or overruled. When you learn how to do this by choice, you can make encouraging improvements leading to positive results. Choices of different behaviors, decisions, and action steps reside in your head.

"A sleeping pill will never take the place of a clear conscience."

-Eddie Cantor

Unfortunately, unchecked self-talk predominantly focuses on short-term decisions. This is vital for the simple reason that self-talk helps you get through life on a minute-by-minute, day-by-day basis. Remember, self-talk is based on sensory input and perceptions, and therefore is ruled more by feelings than logic. The Principles of Noble Intent are more aligned with long-range thinking. This is why we have to train our self-talk to align with Noble Intent. When we do this, our self-talk is the vocal guide for our conscience.

Often the only time our behaviors and actions are not ruled by our self-talk is when we stop to think - consciously - about the long-range or short-term consequences of our actions. This is our conscience mind having a say in how we process what we are going to do. This is your conscience talking.

Your Self-talk is the Internal Vocalization of Your Conscience

If you let your self-talk continue without reining it in consciously, you will more than likely make choices you will live to regret. Without giving your mind clear value-based guidance, your inner voice might convince you to take action according to what 'feels good' in that moment - not necessarily on what is the good, best or noble thing to do.

During times of high pressure and deadlines, some have been guilty of snapping or being short with people. Those who endorse Noble Intent will communicate their apologies because of their conscience.

Self-talk and Internal Dialog

Internal dialog is what you say when you talk to yourself. When you contemplate your world, work through problems, talk through your emotion, recant events, or mull over situations internally, your self-talk helps you sort out your life and makes decisions. It is the way we consider what we need to do. It is the vehicle that allows us to consider choices and weigh options.

Many behavioral scientists make the argument that internal dialog runs continually in your head - which you cannot turn off. They contend that you would not be able to function without it. The bottom line: What you think about and the conversations that you have with yourself will result in actions and behavior. Sometimes, when you are upset the audio track playing in your head will sound angry, annoyed, outraged or irritated as it thrashes out the incident that provoked negative emotions. At other times, your internal dialog will be calm and focused. Your internal dialog will sound composed and thoughtful, introspective and contemplative. It will think objectively and fairly. It will be unselfish and focused on the common good, and it will be in line with those principles you hold dear.

When your internal audio track is tuned into the Principles of Noble Intent, it sounds like channel of communication focused on Noble Intent. This is called Noble Intent Self-talk. How do you make certain that you uphold the Principles of Noble Intent by using your internal dialog? You probably already have an internal audio track that has some Noble Intent thoughts. Now, you need to build upon your current foundation by making certain that you think about your actions and decisions in terms of intentional Noble Intent.

One of the best examples of someone who overcame adversity by using Noble Intent Self-talk was author David Pelzer. If anyone ever had a reason to become an evil, vengeful, even murderous person, it was David Pelzer.

Sometime after he turned four, Pelzer's life became a downward spiral of physical and psychological abuse that, on several occasions, crossed the line into sadism and torture. It started with unprovoked beatings for being a "bad boy" from his emotionally disturbed and alcoholic mother. Before long the beatings escalated. He suffered head contusions, a broken arm, a stabbing in the stomach with a kitchen knife, and having his arm held over the flickering flames of a gas stove. His mother did everything but kill him.

Pelzer was banished to live in the basement where he slept on an army cot. She stripped away his name, calling him 'It' instead of David and made him a slave in his own home. Throughout his autobiographical book, A Child Called 'It', Pelzer reiterated the promise to prove that he is not a "bad boy." After another incident of being stabbed by his mother, Pelzer lay in bed about to give up. Then he remembered the promise he made to himself. The only way she can win, he writes, is if he dies. He became all the more determined to live.

The pep talks Pelzer gave himself - his positive internal dialog - over those awful eight years was his way of self-nurturing. Through positive self-talk, Pelzer found a way to care for himself, to soothe and reassure himself that he was somebody who was worthy of being loved and cared for. Although it would take Pelzer years to finally believe that he was not a "bad boy" and even longer before he stopped wanting to prove his mother wrong, his self-talk kept him going. As an adult, by continuing his positive self-talk, Pelzer managed to lock away the abuse he suffered and became a best selling author, motivational speaker, and a loving father.

Focusing on positive thoughts of how you want your life to be and channeling your internal dialogue toward Principles of Noble Intent is important for everyone to practice. It is also the easiest way to incorporate acting with and assuming Noble Intent into your life. Why? Acting with Noble Intent is something that must come from within you. Assuming Noble Intent is something you talk yourself through. Both are highly dependent on your skill at channeling your self-talk toward Noble Intent.

How can self-talk facilitate acting with Noble Intent?

Think of self-talk and acting with Noble Intent as connected muscles. The more you exercise them, the stronger each becomes individually and as a unit. The link between self-talk and acting with Noble Intent will not happen overnight, but if you buy in to the principles, the rewards will be evident.

"This is the sum of duty: Do not do to others what would cause pain if done to you."

- *Hinduism*, Mahabharata 5:1517

Chapter 8

Linking Noble Intent with Self-talk

"It is not every bad man that will ever be good, but there will be no good man who was not at all some time bad."

-St. Augustine

As you begin practicing Noble Intent, pay close attention to how you react to outside input. As you listen to others, what are you specifically saying to yourself? How is your internal dialog helping or hindering you in keeping with the Principles of Noble Intent? How do you respond to other people's comments when dealing with unpleasant issues? What is your thought process before speaking with a colleague in a potentially unpleasant meeting? What specifically are you saying to yourself? Has your perception been skewed by another person's actions or words? Start listening to the audio track running in your head and make a conscious effort to adjust it if necessary.

> Your self-talk spins off thoughts that form the basis for your decisions and their consequent actions.

How Input from Others Affects Noble Intent

Understanding how other people's messages affect our view of a situation is critical. Let's dissect one of mankind's most fundamental forms of communication - gossip.

Imagine that you have an excellent working relationship with Debra. As an employee she is bright, creative, cooperative, and willing to go the extra mile to get the job done. Since joining your organization, Debra has tackled problems and provided solutions. You are nothing short of thrilled with her work and trust her judgment and leadership.

One afternoon you meet Al and Mike for lunch. The three of you start discussing employees. At the mention of Debra's name, Al gets a look like the mayo on his sandwich was left out overnight under a warming lamp. "I promoted Debra to team leader last year and after I promoted her, she made my job as the department head very difficult," Al offers without anyone asking.

"Why?" you ask innocently. Al casts a quick glance at Mike and then to you. He puts down his sandwich and begins. "Well, Debra and Greg, my peers in the marketing department, really hit it off. They just took the team and started running with it. In fact, it wasn't long before I was being left out of the loop. Before I made Debra team leader, she ran everything by me. I had to travel quite a bit during the project, which was fine. But what I didn't like was that when they knew I was away, they would co-sponsor meetings and set the agenda together. What was worse was trying to find out what happened while I was gone. It was like pulling teeth to get them to give me all the details."

"Wow," you say, trying to defend your employee, "That really doesn't sound like Debra at all!"

"And you'll love this," Al says looking at you and ignoring your last comment. "Some of the meetings that I couldn't attend, they actually scheduled it so that my other peers could come. I felt like they were usurping my authority and keeping me away from team decisions. I got suspicious and started poking around and asking questions. I found out that the two of them were deeper into the details and decisions than even I thought. They were working together every night until almost midnight for weeks."

"When I joked with Debra that she and Greg were getting pretty friendly, she got real uncomfortable and looked upset. I thought they might be having an affair - even though they were both married at the time. Who knows? Maybe they were because I heard Greg left his wife right around that time. Anyway, Debra asked for a transfer to your department as soon as my project ended. Greg wrote her a recommendation for another promotion - which she got even though I didn't approve it. The VP moved her up again and now somebody twelve years less experienced than two of my other guys is my peer!"

"I was my own worst enemy with her. I helped her and promoted her and then, boom, she left with practically no warning. Some loyalty! The VP looked at my glowing recommendation for the last promotion, plus the fact that Debra and Greg brought the project in two months early. Of course, they were able to do that because they spent all their spare time together. I didn't think she was ready and I don't think it was fair to promote her instead of more experienced guys. Without Greg's help she wouldn't be where she is now. History's full of women who've been promoted the same way. I'm sure she's latched herself onto someone else to help her along."

Gossip - good or bad - is insidious. Why? Because try as you might, you cannot block out everything you hear and that can color your view of the person being gossiped about. Al's diatribe is only his point of view but his words have damaged Debra's image and reputation. If you fail to recalibrate and analyze Al's gossip, chances are you will be wary of Debra. You may stop trusting her. For instance, if she schedules a meeting while you are out of town, you will almost certainly question her motivation and loyalty. You will wonder if she is using your project to further her career, even though you encouraged her to do that. What was a positive has suddenly become a negative. The next thing you know you will be examining Debra's relationships with a jaundiced eye. After all, she is really friendly and attractive and there is a grain of truth in what Al said about some women. Is she really capable of what Al suggested? Could any of what Al said be true?

Using Noble Intent to Re-evaluate and Dismiss Gossip

How can you neutralize the impact of Al's words and make sure that you don't perpetuate the malicious gossip? The answer lies in keeping the Principles of Noble Intent in the forefront of your internal dialog.

Using the Principles of Noble Intent, seek out potential reasons for what Al said Debra did. Let's assume for a moment that everything Al claims happened is true. Could it be that Al just got his perception skewed because he was feeling miffed? Was Debra in fact trying to help Al and the organization? After Al promoted her to team leader, did she think she had the authority to meet with Greg to brainstorm solutions for the team's problems? And perhaps Debra thought the best way to thank Al for promoting her was to work extremely hard and make him feel confident that he made the right decision. Maybe she was just taking all the work on herself because she saw how overloaded Al was. Maybe she was being just the type of self-motivated employee that we all would love to have work for us! And perhaps Debra thought that Al would look good to his managers if the project came in early. Isn't it noble to make others look good? Could it be that Debra has Noble Intent and Al is a jealous boss?

Any way you slice it, Debra has proven that she is a valuable employee. Al may have felt slighted or that he had lost control of the project and Debra's future. Moreover, Al may be a little out of step when it comes to how and when people should be promoted.

Is Al a bad guy? No, not if you believe that most people have Noble Intent - even though they don't always show it! So what was Al's Noble Intent? Well, first he must do a better job of thinking through what he wants to say and how he says it. The fact is, Al may have been concerned about the organization and Debra's best interests. He might think that Debra does not have the depth and experience to warrant her latest promotion. Remember, the VP promoted her on reports from other people. The VP has not worked with her directly. Al has. He knows how she works alone and in team settings. If there are flaws in her work, he has seen them. If she is not ready for the big time and fails, the promotion may be too much too soon and ruin her career.

Most egregious and where Noble Intent was completely absent in Al's tirade, was his attack on Debra and Greg's personal reputations. It is simply unforgivable that someone in his position would insinuate that an employee was, "sleeping their way to the top," not to mention being disloyal to their spouse. The personal smear was compounded by telling his colleagues that he suspected Debra and Greg of committing adultery. It was not only disrespectful and insulting, but highly unprofessional.

One can only hope that whenever you hear someone disparaging anyone in this way, that you will step up to the plate, remembering the Principles of Noble Intent, to try to stop this type of insidious gossip. Always do your best to rebuke disparaging remarks and innuendo or censure reputation-ruining rumors.

Noble Intent is Not Always Present

Critical Differentiation Factors - Noble Intent versus Malicious Intent

For everything light, there is a dark side. In Noble Intent, the first and most important question you must ask yourself is: Based on available evidence, is this person trying to help me or do they have malicious intent? This critical differentiation factor will set in motion two oppositional ways of thinking about the situation or the people involved. As you might imagine, the answer will determine how you deal with the event.

Rest assured that most people do not operate from a position of malicious intent. The vast majority of people are not hateful, spiteful, malevolent, mean, nasty, cruel or wicked. And popular conspiracy theories aside, most people are not plotting how best to stick it to you. Nor are they out to get you. These people do exist and you must be aware that some people are indeed malicious in their intent. The unfortunate consequence of dealing with a lot of people is that the more people you deal with, the more you will come across these ignoble individuals. That being said, our experience tells us that these people are rare. In fact, the vast majority of people are quite the opposite. We would venture that an overwhelming majority of people want to help, not hinder, your progress.

That does not mean, however, that good people will not do things that are clearly contrary to Principles of Noble Intent. Nor will they always behave in a manner that represents the values of Noble Intent. We are, after all, human beings and we have been known to be spiteful and petty for no discernable reason. Sometimes people just do not think about the consequences of their actions. Given a second chance, they most likely would behave more nobly. Even good people with a solid history of acting with Noble Intent can behave poorly from time to time. I know I have. I am guessing if you think real hard, an incident or two may pop into your head. Usually it means that a person who was normally of good character was acting out of fear without really thinking through the long-term ramifications of their actions.

Recently a client, Delia, told me that Paul, someone she had worked with for years and whose friendship and opinion she valued, "publicly threw me and my team under the bus."[2] Delia had several discussions with Paul about adjusting his department's forecast numbers downward. They both knew that the president was going to hit the roof at the next meeting. Paul told Delia that he was going to tell the president that overzealous forecasting by one of his finance guys was the cause. Paul said that would tell their boss that Delia and her team were not responsible for any of the faulty forecasts.

The next day at the meeting Paul stood in front of the president and, stuttering and stammering, blamed the dip in revenue on Delia's team, and completely absolving his own guys. Well, as you might expect, Delia was beyond furious. A person she trusted and considered a friend had acted out of character. She decided not to get mad. She wanted

---

2 The names have been changed to protect privacy.

to get even. Delia planned to "return the favor" during a follow-up meeting called by the president to figure out the reason behind the bad forecasts.

It was right about then that I reminded Delia of her commitment to Noble Intent.

"Would it not be better to call your colleague and give him the opportunity to explain his actions, to undo the damage, and to rectify the problem in front of the President?" I asked.

I suggested that Delia have a candid discussion with Paul. I encouraged her to tell Paul that she understood that he felt he was painted into a corner at the meeting when the readjusted forecast was announced. Also to tell Paul that she was surprised when he blamed her department, particularly after they had so many conversations about this matter. I told her to make it clear that the only reason she did not refute his statement was that she did not want to damage his reputation in front of the president. Nor did she want to potentially destroy the working relationship she had built over the years.

During the discussion Delia put Paul on notice that she was not going to let stand what Paul had reported. But rather than rebutting him publicly, she suggested that he retract his earlier report and offer the real reason for the shortfall in the forecast. Doing so would best serve the division, her relationship and Paul's reputation. If Paul agreed, Delia and Paul could craft a statement together that would help undo the damage. The original intent of putting truthful and realistic figures in front of the management team in a timely manner would then be served.

"None of you [truly] believes until he wishes for his brother what he wishes for himself."

- *Islam*, Number 13 of Imam "Al-Nawawi's Forty Hadiths."

Chapter 9

The Process of Reworking Your Self-talk

We are often unaware of how much our internal voice controls our words and actions. Internal influences play a crucial role in our behavior. If you control your inner voice, you will be able to steer your thoughts and actions toward the Principles of Noble Intent.

If you have determined that the person does not have malicious intent, you must then decide what their basis is for operating with Noble Intent.

Let's look at a few examples of how you can adjust your behavior by correcting your internal voice. If you hear yourself say something like, "I cannot believe I did not deliver that presentation better," or, "I wish I was a better presenter," order yourself to stop the negative statements. Then replace those negative thoughts. Say something like, "The next time I make a presentation, I will do an even better job. I learned a good lesson today about being prepared. I can spend more time with the material so I can answer the questions more effectively. I'll even get a colleague to role-play a question and answer session with me the day before I present." By consistently using your self-nurturing inner dialogue to reinforce acting with Noble Intent, it will become stronger and more instinctive.

Examine the following table to see exactly how this process works. Listen carefully to precisely what you say to yourself. Whenever you find yourself making a critical self-talk statement, or one that does not align with how you have chosen to act, behave or think, stop yourself. Rewind and rephrase the statement in a positive way to leave the negative influence behind just like you see being done in the table. By using a similar pattern, you can turn your internal voice into a positive force to motivate you to become better at incorporating Principles of Noble Intent into your thoughts and behavior.

The process is simple:

1. Listen to the person's exact words.

2. Determine if they would have any potential negative impact on your self-talk if you do not assume and act with Noble Intent.

3. Assume Noble Intent and define what you think the person's Noble Intent is.

4. Recalibrate, reword, rework or reformulate the words so that you adjust your self-talk saying a positive message to yourself.

Example 1

External Input

1. **Coach says:** "You are not scoring points because you do not practice your shots often enough."

2. **Negative impact:** You feel that you are not living up to the coach's standards of how much time you need to get better. You are hurt by the coach's words and become unmotivated or get angry.

Assume Noble Intent and Recalibrate Their Words for Positive Impact in Your Self-talk

3. **Assuming Noble Intent:** My coach wants me to reach my full potential.

4. **What I will say to myself:** "Coach is right. My shots will improve if I practice and listen to what coach says."

Example 2

External Input

1. **Teacher says:** "Ian, if you study harder you will make A's instead of B's."

2. **Negative impact:** You may feel that the teacher is pressuring you beyond what you feel capable of achieving and, therefore, you could choose to say to yourself: "No matter what I do, I may never be quite good enough."

Assume Noble Intent and Recalibrate Their Words for Positive Impact in Your Self-talk

3. **Assuming Noble Intent:** My teacher is so proud of my report card because I've really pulled my grades up. Now, my teacher thinks that an A, something I never believed possible, is possible.

4. **What I will say to myself:** "If I continue studying each afternoon and apply myself, I bet I can earn a few A's on my next report card."

Example 3

External Input

1. **Boss says:** "Jeff, you have way too many great ideas for us to implement."

2. **Negative impact:** If you do not act with Noble Intent, you might refuse to tell anyone about your next idea for fear of overwhelming them. You might feel alienated from the team if you take the comments in the wrong light. Perhaps you could even think that you are unusual and out of the norm. You might conclude that your boss is a jerk assuming that you do not know how to prioritize or effectively put a plan in place. This could affect your relationship with her.

Assume Noble Intent and Recalibrate Their Words for Positive Impact in Your Self-talk

3. **Assuming Noble Intent:** My boss really thinks I have a lot of unique ideas that she likes. She just wishes they had more resources so that the team could actually implement more of my ideas.

4. **What I will say to myself:** "I have to find a way to show my boss how these ideas can be put easily into practice. They don't need to be accomplished all at once. I will prioritize my ideas and put the best ones into a timetable so that she can understand my plan better. This way we can implement all of my ideas to improve the organization over time."

Example 4

External Input

1. **Colleague says:** "Your presentation would have been better if you had been better prepared."

2. **Negative impact:** This is particularly negative because of people's fear of speaking in front of others. It also assumes that another person knows what is causing you to falter. But preparation may not be your problem. The solution may be as simple as altering your self-talk about your fear of public speaking.

Assume Noble Intent and Recalibrate Their Words for Positive Impact in Your Self-talk

3. **Assuming Noble Intent:** I saw Curtis smiling during my talk so I know he thinks my speaking skills have improved over the past six months. He really liked when I used one of the tips he taught me.

4. **What I will say to myself:** "I am going to continue to improve. I will prepare more, practice more, and I will continue to ask people for tips and ask for constructive feedback."

Example 5

External Input

1. **Friend says:** "Yolanda, you are way too nice."

2. **Negative impact:** You doubt your way of thinking and, therefore, change your attitude toward people, becoming suspicious and cynical.

Assume Noble Intent and Recalibrate Their Words for Positive Impact in Your Self-talk

3. **Assuming Noble Intent:** My friend respects the fact that I am a nice person. What they meant to say was... You are a very nice person and I don't want Joe to take advantage of your good nature.

4. **What I will say to myself:** "They think I am a nice person but they are worried that people might take advantage of my good nature. I accept their viewpoint. But I am putting out good intentions to the people I have to deal with and am not being naïve. I am hoping that by being nice, the other people in turn will be a bit nicer to me and my team members."

Example 6

External Input

1. **Teammate says:** "I wish you wouldn't always be so friendly, nice, or concerned about the guys in the IT department." (This applies to any label that describes you based on someone else's view of how you should act towards other employees.)

2. **Negative impact:** Your team member may influence you to conform to their current behavior of not cooperating with the IT department. Allowing their way of thinking to change how you act might not help the organization.

Assume Noble Intent and Recalibrate Their Words for Positive Impact in Your Self-talk

3. **Assuming Noble Intent:** Assume that the other person has your best interest at heart. They might be worried about your well-being, your stress, or are looking out for you because the IT department has been behaving poorly. They might think that by treat-

ing IT the way IT treats others is the best way to modify the IT employees' behavior.

4. **What I will say to myself:** "They care about me and that is why they are asking me to be careful about my interactions with the IT department. This is based on their history with people there and not on my experience. I will look at the situation from their eyes and see what I might be missing. However, I am going to be cooperative and keep an open mind."

Example 7

External Input

1. **Another employee says:** "You can't do that! Mike in accounting did that recently and his boss gave him a hard time afterwards. Make sure you don't step outside of your authority. People here won't like it."

2. **Negative impact:** By listening to this person, you might decide to hold back and "wait for permission" to change things in your team, to keep the status quo, and not rock the boat. The result: You were hired because you are a change agent who gets things done and now you will disappoint your boss because you have allowed the current cultural constraints to negatively affect your performance.

Assume Noble Intent and Recalibrate Their Words for Positive Impact in Your Self-talk

3. **Assuming Noble Intent:** They are just trying to warn me to make sure I don't overstep my boundaries and get in trouble.

4. **What I will say to myself:** "I understand what they are saying but I think this is the best course of action. Just because something didn't work in one area doesn't necessarily mean it won't work here. We operate differently from the management philosophy that he was alluding to in the other department. For us, this way of doing things will work and will not have similar negative repercussions. The risk to me personally is worth the reward for the company. I was hired to push the envelope and shake things up around here and make them better."

Chapter 10

Noble Intent & Your Reputation

By channeling your thoughts toward the Principles of Noble Intent, you will build a strong force that will direct your inner voice. As you go through life, your inner voice creates your conscience and this becomes the force that guides your behavior.

> Conscience is that still, small voice
> That quells a wicked thought
> Then adds this sequence,
> 'Besides, you'll get caught.'
> Supervision

Some people only think with their conscience when they are personally threatened. Others live their lives through their conscience. For the past 30 years, Rick Frishman has worked in the hyper-kinetic New York public relations market where it is no exaggeration to say hyperbole is standard. Yet amidst the fierce competition for clients, Frishman has not only managed to preserve his integrity and reputation, he is renowned for it.

"The reputation is your most important attribute," said Frishman, president of Planned TV Arts, a division of Ruder Finn that specializes in publicity for authors, entrepreneurs, and businesses. "Once you ruin your reputation, it is hard to get back."

A prolific author and speaker, Frishman has kept on track with the straight and narrow by relying on the lessons learned at his parents' knees and the wisdom passed down from his business mentor. Those dogmas included treating people well and with kindness, being careful about what you say about other people, and always taking the high road. Frishman was essentially

"Conscience and reputation are two things. Conscience is due to yourself, reputation to your neighbor."

St. Augustine:
Works, Vol. XXI

"A man should wander about treating all creatures as he himself would be treated."

- *Jainism,*
Sutrakritanga
1.11.33

being taught to act with, and assume Noble Intent. And now, it rules his conscience.

"You learn (Noble Intent) from your parents and how they treat each other, their children and others," he said. "People care about being respected, loved and also like feeling that what they do matters."

Labor to keep alive in your breast that little spark of celestial fire, called Conscience.

Frishman has always treated his employees and clients with Noble Intent. His conscience won't allow anything less. He is upfront with clients, saying that somewhere along the line something will go wrong. His advice, if it does, is to "Own up to it and take care of it."

"The problem comes if you hide it or make up excuses or cover up," he said. "It goes to integrity and good business. The two most powerful words in business are 'I'm sorry'."

But it also speaks to an individual's character. Before Frishman hires a colleague or accepts a client, he often will take them to lunch, not to observe their table manners, but to see how they treat the waiter.

"Watch how someone treats a person who can't help them in any way," he said. "That will tell you about their character. People want to deal with sane and nice people, by and large. If you are crazy and treat people poorly, nobody wants you around."

Frishman has always treated members of his team well. In fact, he avoids calling the people who work with him employees. Rather, they are his colleagues or associates. He stresses to each and every one of them the value he places on doing the right thing.

"I tell them straight out: 'I am very proud of you and that you have always done great work in doing the right thing for our clients. Always act the right way, with integrity.'"

"Labor to keep alive in your breast that little spark of celestial fire, called Conscience."

-George Washington: Moral Maxims: Conscience

"No hell like a bad conscience."

-John Crowne: The Ambitious Statesman, Act V, scene 3

Nor does Rick Frishman want his people working for clients who make them uncomfortable or whom they feel are not right for Planned TV Arts. Those issues are sometimes the topics at the agency's Ethics Committee meetings. The committee, which invites priests, ministers and rabbis to discuss vexing business issues, has been around since the 1940s, according to Frishman.

"Number one, my employees need to know that in any situation we will do the right thing," Frishman said. "We will always refund a client's money if there is a question. We will always act with integrity. They see that we do the right thing. They want to know they are at a place that has a heart. If they see you doing bad things to people, they feel dirty."

Frishman agrees with Noble Intent adherents that most people are good and want to do what is right. But when problems arise, he has seen too many executives revert to their old thinking. That can leave middle-level managers torn about what to do. Noble Intent flows from the top. It must be the company's acknowledged value system under which it operates.

"The problem is the people at the middle management level are afraid about losing their jobs," he said. "It is a very hard thing. When do you become the whistle blower? When do you stand up to your boss and say, 'This is not right. I am not going to do it.' That is where people have the most problems."

In today's instant information environment, an employee irked by a company's ethical conduct can have a major impact. One online post is all it takes to publicly expose a company's collection of skeletons.

"You have to be careful because there are no secrets in the world," he said. "I always tell people, 'If you have done something bad, one person at your company can post it and tell the world in 30 seconds. If there is something bad to be said, it is much better that you own up to it, say you screwed up and apologize.' Then people move on."

Your Conscience and Your Reputation

People use their conscience unfailingly to guide their self-talk and, therefore, their behavior. If you align your self-talk and conscience with Noble Intent tenets, you will make certain your reputation stays in line with Principles of Noble Intent and to build trust with others.

Leadership and Visualization

Leadership with Noble Intent insists that you create an environment whereby the Principles of Noble Intent can be nurtured and grown. Audio is to self-talk what video is to visualization. Self-talk is thinking about the script writing in your own mind. Visualization is directing the scene.

Visualization is another way to make acting with Noble Intent part of your daily life. As we talked about in an earlier chapter, visualization is the mental image of an event or situation that runs like a movie in your mind. Since you are the writer, director and actor, the movie plays out the way you want it to in real life. Don't forget - you also have complete authority over the words that you add to your video. Remember to use the lessons of powerful self-talk when creating your visualizations. Visualization's job is to introduce the brain to a particular pattern of thinking. Once again, the more you exercise the muscle, the stronger it gets. So if you imagine acting with Noble Intent, your brain will be primed to follow through when the time comes. Everyone from professional athletes to brain surgeons practices visualization before a big game or operation. They put themselves in the moment, conjuring up the sights, sounds, and even the smells to make the exercise in the process of visualization as realistic as possible. Then they walk through every motion, step by step.

You can use visualization before a client appointment or department meeting. Visualization can help you prepare for challenges from people who are threatened because you act with Noble Intent. Teaching acting with Noble Intent using a self-nurturing inner dialogue and visualization works for individuals. Now let's talk about how you as a leader, can convey the message of acting with Noble Intent to your corporation.

"There is a difference between him who does no misdeeds because of his own conscience and him who is kept from wrong-doing because of the presence of others."

-The Talmud

Chapter 11

Acting with Noble Intent:
How Corporations Do It

"Lucifer, I have 5 CEO's and 3 CFO's I need you to sign for."

DeadEx Delivering Dead Executives

Many hold corporations and their executives in questionable esteem. The general public believes corporations are money-grubbing, bottom-line driven monoliths. If the choice comes down to cash or principles, many believe that large corporations are inherently incapable of acting with Noble Intent.

The reality, of course, is strikingly different. Business has come a long way since the slash and burn policies of the last century. The list of Fortune 500 companies acting with Noble Intent is steadily growing. Even companies that once had terrible reputations as a result of questionable practices have managed to turn them around. For example, many of America's most profitable companies have been attacked in recent years for their labor practices in the developing world. Realizing that not adhering to the Principles of Noble Intent was impacting their potential profits, Liz Claiborne, Reebok, New Balance, and Timberland Co., just to name a few, have all voluntarily changed their labor codes of conduct and they have all experienced exceptional profit increases since.

The Principles of Noble Intent Work Successfully in Profitable Businesses

Perhaps the best modern example of Noble Intent in business is the Grameen Bank founded by Muhammad Yunus. The Norwegian Nobel Committee decided to Award Muhammad Yunus and the Grameen Bank the Nobel Peace Prize for 2006. The press release by the Nobel Committee stated "Muhammad Yunus has shown himself to be a leader who has managed to translate visions into practical action for the benefit of millions of people, not only in Bangladesh, but also in many other countries."

The concept of fiscally-responsible loans to poor people without any financial security had appeared to be a money-foolish idea for a bank to adopt. From modest beginnings three decades ago, Yunus developed micro-credit into an important instrument in the struggle against poverty. Grameen Bank has been a source of ideas and is a model for the many institutions in the field of micro-credit that have sprung up around the world. The Noble Intent concept that prevails is Yunus's long-term vision to eliminate poverty in the world. Micro-credit has proved to be an important liberating force in societies where women in particular have to struggle against repressive social and economic conditions.

Grameen realized that the typical way of doing banking business was not incompatible with its social mission. Yunus was the leader of his organization and he knew that helping the poor is no excuse for not running a good business. Because Grameen wanted to be both an efficient business and serve the poor, it worked to design (and redesign) policies and procedures as well as employee incentive structures that rewarded - sometimes in a precarious balance - these goals. Grameen's unusual ability to do this appears to derive from its founder and his recognition that doing good is not easy.

Institution building with the Principles of Noble Intent has no "right" formula, aside from making it a conscious and continuous part of the strategic plan. In short, Grameen proved that it can be profitable while carrying out a noble, Nobel Award winning mission.

Other highly-successful corporations, with less visible or compelling social missions, have retooled their corporate images by working for the greater good of their stakeholders, customers, employees and communities. Goldman Sachs, for instance, has created an Urban Investment Group whose goal is "becoming the preferred provider of investment capital to ethnic minority businesses and urban real estate ventures." Rest assured, Goldman Sachs would not make an investment of this kind if it did not provide a return on investment.

While many companies have changed their ways or enhanced their practices to fall into alignment with Noble Intent, others have been built on the Principles of Noble Intent, and in doing so have brought tremendous profits to their stakeholders. Take for example Ben and Jerry's. We know Ben and Jerry's to have bold, fun flavors palatable to any ice cream connoisseur. Unfortunately, many of us are unaware of their Noble Intent corporate goals. Take a look at Ben and Jerry's three-part mission statement which is "founded on and dedicated to a sustainable corporate concept of linked prosperity":

Product Mission	Economic Mission	Social Mission
To make, distribute & sell the finest quality all natural ice cream & euphoric concoctions with a continued commitment to incorporating wholesome, natural ingredients and promoting business practices that respect the Earth and the environment.	To operate the Company on a sustainable financial basis of profitable growth, increasing value for our stakeholders & expanding opportunities for development and career growth for our employees.	To operate the company in a way that actively recognizes the central role that business plays in society by initiating innovative ways to improve the quality of life locally, nationally & internationally.

Ben and Jerry's, a homegrown company in Vermont, was so profitable and had so much potential, that the giant Unilever purchased it in 2000 with one caveat: that Ben & Jerry's "join forces with Unilever to create an even more dynamic, socially positive ice cream business with a much more global reach."

These examples of well-known companies represent only a small portion of enterprises which adopt Principles of Noble Intent and continue to develop their messages and profits based on its tenets. It is clearly paying off for them. Each of these companies devised conscientious objectives to adopt Noble Intent, with the specific goals inherent in profitable enterprises. Interestingly, each enterprise created vastly differing strategies to meet their objectives.

Commercials with a Conscience

For some families, living with Noble Intent is like an heirloom that is passed down from one generation to the next. Children learn the importance of treating others with kindness, respect and understanding through the example of their elders.

Lise Avery grew up in one of those families. The producer and voice behind the microphone of the syndicated radio program, Anything Goes, Avery remembers the enormous weight the twin ideas of personal integrity and responsibility held by her parents. So impressed was she that those two principles became the pilings upon which she erected her value system of Noble Intent.

"I don't really know that I can pinpoint a moment that was an epiphany for me," said Avery, who is also a singer and actor. "I just find that as I grow and mature that Noble Intent becomes stronger within me and I find myself surrounded by like-minded people. I am fortunate to have close friends and compatriots who believe the same thing. Having people trust and believe in you, you cannot put a monetary value on that."

Avery has found that Noble Intent is not only an

"Man's chief purpose… is the creation and preservation of values; that is what gives meaning to our civilization, and the participation in this is what gives significance, ultimately, to the individual human life."

-Lewis Mumford

immensely rewarding value system, but also a dynamic energy that draws people to her. Even on the telephone Avery exudes the aura of someone who understands what is important, who is a successful human being.

Avery also values creative freedom, so she made the decision to work in syndication radio. Her show, Anything Goes, is an expression of her belief in Noble Intent. "I am fortunate in that by producing my own program I am in a bubble," she said. Radio station managers "cannot fire me. They can drop me from the broadcast schedule, but they cannot tell me what I can and cannot say or which music I am going to play."

Anything Goes does not accept traditional buy-this-product type ads - no exception. The policy, what she calls "Commercials With a Conscience," has been in place since Day 1. She adopted it because Anything Goes is so closely identified with her. The show is her concept, her musical taste, and her voice on most of the commercial spots. Advertisers who want air time on Anything Goes must write ad copy that informs rather than sells.

"The nature and intent is to change the course of commercial media and it is beginning to happen," she said. "It was a matter of putting words to a belief system. It is about creating a message that has value in the world rather than just buy, buy, buy." she said. "With almost any company you can name there is an issue that is beneficial for the consumer to know about that the company can get behind.

"I take my responsibility as a member of the media, even a small one, very, very seriously. I conclude each radio program by saying, `Be kind to yourself, each other and the earth'," she said. "I have had that repeated back to me by my listeners." No doubt her message is getting through. Her show is aired in fourteen markets in the Northeastern United States.

Chapter 12

Self-Actualization and Personal Fulfillment through Noble Intent

If you are interested in finding how to go about attaining personal fulfillment, a good place to start is Abraham Maslow's Theory of Self-Actualization. Maslow presented his theory of human motivation in 1943. The hierarchy, also known as the Hierarchy of Needs, is built on the premise that people naturally yearn to reach self-fulfillment, what Maslow calls Self-Actualization. It is the pinnacle of his pyramid. But self-actualization is unattainable until our basic needs are fulfilled.

The pyramid is dynamic. In order to attain self-actualization, we must hold true to Maslow's principles. We learn from life experiences as we ascend through the levels of the pyramid. When we go against our value system, we create stress.

"Habits change into character."

-Ovid

MASLOW'S HIERARCHY
INDABA

Fulfillment Needs
Self-Fulfillment
Self-Actualization

Relationship Needs
Esteem
Self respect & feelings of success
Achievement
(According to societal norms)
love & feelings of belonging

Existence Needs
Safety
(Security, Order, Stability)
Physiological Needs
(Hunger, Thirst, Shelter, Body comforts, Heat, etc.

Wendy Reid Crisp, a writer and the current editor of GRAND, the magazine for grandparents, learned the consequences of acting in conflict with her values.

When Nobel Intent became a part of the life of Crisp, it was not a conscious choice. Crisp began her career in 1965 as a receptionist/editorial assistant for a computer magazine in Los Angeles. The staff was "the smartest, finest bunch of people" she has ever met. It was also her first brush with what she would come to recognize as Noble Intent. "They taught me everything that was important about jobs and life," she said. "They all took a huge interest in me."

Crisp became the editor-in-chief of Savvy in 1981. While the new magazine had proven quite successful with a number of top women executives, the publisher wanted to reach women in all stages of management careers. As editor, Crisp infused it with a new vision of success, one that included community responsibilities and lifelong learning; the circulation of the magazine increased from 100,000 to 400,000 within three years.

"Savvy gave me a platform to honor the whole philosophy that I came with, that is, honoring the lives of people as they are, rather than giving them a strange media image that minimizes their lives," she said. "I got in trouble a lot."

Regardless of how well the magazine did, Crisp was constantly challenged on content by the publisher and by the magazine's distributors. Yet she held fast. That is, until the magazine was sold. The new publisher nearly doubled her salary, gave her a fabulous office and unbelievable perks. Everything was fine until the new publisher decided to change the magazine's look and content. Crisp, seduced by the perks and the money, went along with the program without much objection.

One day, stranded briefly at an airport without her limo, Crisp called her assistant and threw what she describes as a 'hissy fit.' When she hung up, she couldn't believe what she had just done. "I thought, what has happened to me?" she said. "Where did that obnoxious sense of entitlement come from?"

"I had become someone I could not respect," she said. "I had sold my soul. I was not doing work I was proud of. I had sold out totally. I was going down the drain and I hadn't even noticed it." Her business success had come at the cost of her Noble Intent principles, a price she was unwilling to pay. A month later, she quit.

It took her eight years to get back on her feet. Still, she never once regretted leaving. In the years since, she has had an eclectic mix of personal and professional successes and failures. The successes have been her three books of humor, on turning 50, raising good children despite being a less-than-perfect mother, and turning 60. She has also written and produced documentary films; hosted two radio shows; edited magazines, written articles, worked as a volunteer in women's prisons, and raised thousands of dollars for educational and social welfare work in her community and as president of the charitable non-profit, San Francisco-based Institute for Family Development International, for women and children in the United States and Africa.

Initially, Crisp did not call her value system Noble Intent. Frankly, the word combination would have never occurred to her. But now that she knows what Noble Intent means, she likes the phrase. It defines her values.

"It is good that the phrase exists," she said. "That is a step forward. It is like the word diversity, the kinds of concepts that didn't exist when I was 20 and starting out in the business world. Noble Intent's real power," she believes, "comes from people who take pride in their work and who value the respect of others."

Where are your people on the pyramid?

Before teaching your employees how to act with Noble Intent, guess where each person is on Maslow's Hierarchy. Are they in conflict? Do your organization's core values align with theirs? Does the change you are going through work with their ideals? Depending on their current pyramid position, people will likely react differently to what you are proposing. Remember, you are asking people to change, something human beings don't like or do easily. But more than just change, you are asking them to alter - and in some cases abandon - a personal value system that has developed over a lifetime.

As the leader you must recognize what each employee needs to be able to accept acting with Noble Intent. Probe for prior bad experiences, such as a run-in with a boss that may make someone unreceptive to acting with Noble Intent. Realize and acknowledge that everyone has some personal biases to overcome. Try to identify built-in patterns of human behavior, such as natural fears and phobias, and other potential learned (nature/nurture) reactions.

Leadership is invaluable when teaching people to act with Noble Intent. Remember, change and people equals fear. People act differently when they are afraid. If fear is high, the chances of anyone acting with Noble Intent are low. People must feel comfortable to be open to change.

Go back to Maslow's Hierarchy and make sure everyone's existence and relationship needs have been met. Then tell people the company is embarking on an exciting new way of doing business that focuses on the greater good of the employees, the company and the community. Most people will buy in because they want to be a part of something bigger than them and work for the greater good. They want to achieve and enjoy self-respect and success. It's natural instinct.

Tell your employees that acting with Noble Intent is a major part of your personal and professional value system. Explain that acting with Noble Intent for you means believing that if you expect the best from people, they will give you their best.

Noble Intent in the corporate setting means helping other departments, even if it doesn't advance an agenda. Let's say your department is doing well but another department is cash strapped and can't complete its project. Acting with Noble Intent means finding a way to help the department for the greater good of the company and client. It wasn't until the members of the Constitutional Congress put aside their individual agendas and began acting with Noble Intent that the enduring document that guides our country was hammered out. You might say that America was built on acting with Noble Intent.

Team Leadership and Noble Intent

As the team leader, remind people daily that the department always acts with Noble Intent. Begin meetings by saying it's required that everyone act with Noble Intent. Before ending meetings check to make sure that you acted with Noble Intent on every decision. Put up "Act with Noble Intent" signs around the office to remind people. Add a line about acting with Noble Intent in your e-mails. Name a Noble Intent employee of the month - give that person a small award. The goal is to make acting with Noble Intent automatic and rewarding.

If you have the power, weave acting with Noble Intent into the company's fabric. Insert a section in the handbook about acting with Noble Intent to further solidify its importance. Make it as clear as a sunny, spring morning that you expect each and every person you supervise to act with Noble Intent in dealing with you, each other, outside departments and clients. As long

"The career of a great man reminds an enduring monument of human energy. The man dies and disappears, but his thoughts and acts survive and leave an indelible stamp upon his race."

-Samuel Smiles

"... thou shalt love thy neighbor as thyself."

- *Judaism*, Leviticus 19:18

as you are sitting in the power seat, there will be no exceptions to the rule.

A friend of Bob Calandra is chairman of the Department of Otolaryngology at The Children's Hospital of Philadelphia. The extremely busy and profitable 70-employee department is run based on acting with Noble Intent. My friend takes a moment with each new employee to explain how the department conducts business, and how he expects them to act when working for him.

"It's important to me that everyone works together and that everyone is treated well and fairly," said William P. Potsic, MD, MMM. "Treating people well pays off in the commitment to the department and each other. If I, as the chairman, treat everyone with respect, then everyone else has to treat each other with respect. It comes out of the culture and is part of the humanity of our department."

Finally, if you are not acting with Noble Intent, allow your employees to call you on it. If you were not acting with Noble Intent, admit it and then examine why that happened. Everyone will learn from the discussion.

"It's easy to dodge our responsibilities, but we cannot dodge the consequences of dodging our responsibilities."

-Sir Josiah Stamp

Chapter 13

Assuming Noble Intent

Now we move on to the concept of assuming Noble Intent. To assume Noble Intent is the heavy lifting part of the Noble Intent concept. Assuming Noble Intent is based on the underlying principle that if you assume the best of people, they will match or exceed your expectations. When you assume Noble Intent, you are presuming that the individual is operating within the Principles of Noble Intent. Every time you assume Noble Intent you make a leap of faith by presupposing that the person is acting with Noble Intent. Please remember that we are not naïve. We realize that not everyone acts with Noble Intent. But isn't it better to first give oth-

"Ideals are like stars: You will not succeed in touching them with your hands, but like the seafaring man on the ocean desert of waters, you choose them as your guides, and following them, you reach your destiny."

-Carl Schurz

Trust earns trust.

ers the benefit of the doubt? Isn't it better to assume that they might be like you and are trying to do the best they can and are working towards a goal? Assuming Noble Intent is logical if you truly believe that the vast majority of people are good - not evil or malicious.

We are going to assume that you believe that assuming Noble Intent is a prudent thing to do. But why don't we automatically assume Noble Intent? This is difficult to do because we are naturally cautious. Perhaps assuming Noble Intent is difficult for you to do because of your experiences in life or in particular with this individual and do not want to be hurt, disappointed or caught unawares. You will notice that these thoughts are self-centered. We have found that the biggest challenge facing people who want to consistently assume Noble Intent is learning how to retrain their thoughts. They must learn to consistently and consciously shift their perspective from internal to external, from self-centered and self-protective to acknowledging and digesting the other person's point of view. They have to make this (shift to the assumption of Noble Intent) a habit. This is particularly difficult when it appears to conflict with their expectations of how others will act. These expectations are formed primarily from the observer's beliefs and experiences.

Before applying the concept of assuming Noble Intent professionally, you should master it personally.

That assumption is often a difficult leap of faith for some individuals to make. The idea of trusting someone to do the right thing - especially when doing the right thing involves no personal gain on their part - grates against our natural instincts and too often it grates against negative nurtured experiences from our past. None of us wants to be considered naïve, or even worse, an easy mark. No one likes to be vulnerable so our natural instincts are defensive. When you are defensive it is difficult to be in the correct Noble Intent mindset.

"There are habits, not only of drinking, swearing, and lying, but of every modification of action, speech, and thought. Man is a bundle of habits; in a word, there is not a quality or function, either of body or mind, which does not feel the influence of this great law of animated nature."

-William Paley

"I will speak ill of no man, and speak all the good I know of everybody."

-Benjamin Franklin

Being defensive means that you are - by definition - being suspicious, self-protective, cynical, distrustful, guarded, skeptical, or disbelieving. None of these promote the openness required when you assume Noble Intent. Even worse, if you put yourself in an offensive or aggressive mindset, one in which you are going to "get them before they get me," it is almost impossible to put yourself in the correct frame of mind to assume Noble Intent.

"There is so much good in the worst of us,

And so much bad in the best of us,

That it ill behooves any of us

To find fault with the rest of us."

-Anonymous

Chapter 14

Noble Intent Cycle

Another way to look at the two sides of Noble Intent is by examining the Noble Intent Cycle. Visually, the cycle demonstrates the relationship between you and another person. If I (ME) observe your actions and behavior (YOU), I can then assume Noble Intent (even though it may go against my perception). That assumption leads to motivations and decisions that influence my behavior and cause you to make observations that may be inconsistent with your perceptions and assumptions.

The Pygmalion effect is a well-researched demonstration of how assuming Noble Intent can be a positive force in your relationships and leadership. The Pygmalion effect is the effect people's expectations have on others' behaviors. At its simplest, people tend to live up, or down, to the expectations others have of them. So, the assumption of Noble Intent communicates an expectation which leads to people living up to that expectation by acting with Noble Intent.

Noble Intent Cycle Model

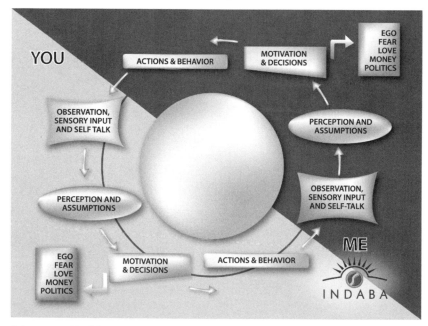

We asked General Alexander, Director, National Security Agency, Chief, Central Security Service (NSA/CSS), "How do you find Noble Intent in an organization?" He said, "You must have awareness of what the organization looks like several layers deep without solely depending on others to give you that view. Other people's views are colored by their personal perceptions, views, motivations and goals." General Alexander cautions against seeing what others want you to see, as that view will be colored by their reality and perceptions. Thus, he is a huge advocate of 'management by walking around' (MBWA). He expects his senior leadership to do the same. "You can't lead an organization from an ivory tower, and if you do, you will steer it wrong. How do you engender personal courage in others? How do you create a culture where people can talk to you and open up? This is a great challenge."

How do you get people to act with personal courage after they may have been taught or have experience that such actions don't serve them well? First and foremost, you have to interact with them personally and they need to know that you value their honest opinions, advice, and input.

Understanding Motivation from the Other Person's Perspective

Begin with the other person's motivation, which can stem from ego, fear, love or money to beliefs and politics. These components are largely responsible for our behavior. If you are inspired to do a good job, your motivation factor may be pride in your accomplishments or it could be fear of losing your job. This depends <u>upon whether your motivation is positive or negative.</u>

For instance, a manager who assumes individual performance is important for career advancement and promotion, might try to make himself look good, even at the company's expense. A savvy leader versed in the Noble Intent Cycle Model knows the manager is driven by one of the factors in the motivation part of the cycle. Assuming Noble Intent, the Noble Intent leader responds as if the manager is trying to do the right thing, but has overlooked an important factor. The Noble Intent Leader counsels the manager to look at his/her behavior from the enterprise viewpoint.

Bemused by the leader's reaction, the manager must reconcile the difference between his selfish actions and the supervisor's expectations that he act with Noble Intent. Most likely through a deeper understanding of another's position, the manager's motivation will change to match the boss' judgment and perception.

In the real world it is certainly possible to do what's right and to be self-serving. Most of us think people are either fair, loyal and trusting team players, or rule-benders looking out for number one. They feel that it is not possible to be self serving and at the same time do the right thing. This isn't necessarily true. Sure, for some, Noble Intent is an impossible concept to practice because their intentions are rarely, if ever, noble.

First Assume Noble Intent on a Small Scale

Your best bet is to start assuming Noble Intent on a small scale, say around your house or when working with someone at work. After all, kindness, understanding and a willingness to sacrifice for the greater good should start with those closest to you. Open yourself to new ways of thinking about your day-to-day interactions. Here again, internal self-talk and dialogue will work well in nailing down the concept. The next time you think that someone is doing something petty or you assume they are trying to slight you, assume Noble Intent. Tell yourself that they did not intentionally mean to hurt or offend you. Let your Noble Intent self-talk programming kick into gear.

The next time you and your spouse have a disagreement try to assume Noble Intent on their part. See what happens? Does it change how you would have typically interacted? Perhaps you think that your spouse is taking a totally unreasonable stance and the 'give and take' is on the verge of escalating into a full-fledged blowout. By looking at the Noble Intent Cycle Model, you can work through the process to defuse the situation. Your attention should be focused on discovering the reason behind your spouse's position. Start with your observations. What are you seeing, hearing and sensing about your spouse's behaviors, actions, feelings, decisions, and motivations? Work through your Noble Intent self-talk.

Ask yourself, "Am I letting my preconceived biases interfere with my judgment of this particular situation? Is my perception open to assuming Noble Intent of my spouse?"

If you keep these questions in the forefront of your mind, you are more likely to keep an open mind. If you consistently do this, your assump-

"To live in the presence of great truths and eternal laws, to be led by permanent ideals - that is what keeps a man patient when the world ignores him, and calm and unspoiled when the world praises him."

-A.P. Peabody

"For attractive lips, speak words of kindness. For lovely eyes, seek out the good in people. For poise, walk in the knowledge that you'll never walk alone."

-Audrey Hepburn

tions will fall more in line with those focused on assuming Noble Intent. In this way, you will form the habit of assuming Noble Intent. Assumptions are an important constituent of decision making. In the Noble Intent Cycle, make certain that you test your assumptions before taking action on them.

Erroneous assumptions based on negative judgments are one of the major reasons people fail to assume Noble Intent. If you truly believe that people are working toward their version of Noble Intent, make certain that your assumptions of their views are on target. To do this, you must test your assumptions. The best way to do this is to ask questions and clarify your insights. Keep an open mind. Be prepared to view the situation from various angles to provide further insight. If you fail, the consequences may be dire. Remember the incident in The Childhood of a Leader, where Jean Paul Sartre told of Lucien, the man who beat a Jewish man and became anti-Semitic because of his friends erroneous assumptions of his motivation.

Noble Intent Tactic

Think "out of the box" and resist assuming that the behavior that you are observing is a manifestation of a negative or harmful purpose. Create realistic and plausible scenarios in your own mind that are based on an assumption of Noble Intent. Now that you have tested your assumptions, you can make decisions based on the facts as you see them. So, instead of confronting an otherwise difficult situation in which there is only one reason a person could possibly be behaving in the manner you observe, there are two or possibly three reasons, with only one reason being possibly nefarious. Decide to assume Noble Intent.

Use a logical decision-making process that can withstand your after-action review. Will you feel good tomorrow about the decisions you are making today? Your rationale for making the decisions should be logical and you must be able

"Cowardice asks, Is it safe? Expediency asks, Is it politic? Vanity asks, Is it popular? But the Conscience asks, Is it right?"

-William Morley Punshon

to succinctly communicate these to others.

Ask yourself: What is motivating me in this situation? Are my reasons for doing this in line with the Principles of Noble Intent?

Motivations/values that are in line with Noble Intent include:		
Helping people reach goals	Love of friends	Challenge
Trust	Peace of mind	Equality
Democracy	Love of family	Power
Education	Love of life partner	Creativity
Honesty	Beauty	Financial success
Success	Mutual communication	Religious faith
Overall security	Respect of peers	Spiritual unity
Respect of friends	Respect of family	Freedom of choice
Financial freedom	Integrity	Personal growth
Helping peers	Sharing knowledge	Teaching others

The next step in the Noble Intent Cycle is exhibited in your actions and behaviors. This is when you act with Noble Intent.

Let's look at your partner's side of the Noble Intent Cycle Model. If you work diligently through the Noble Intent Cycle, any steps your spouse sees as positive might affect their side of the cycle. Small positive considerations may alter their perception of how they think about the situation, too. This could positively impact their side of the Noble Intent Cycle Model. Because they now view this as positive, their perception, assumptions, self-talk, motivation, decisions and finally their actions and behaviors can change for the better.

Bottom line: Your contributions to the process are seen as accepting by your partner and they are compelled to match your Noble Intent, independent of their original motivation.

Over time, once your spouse recognizes that you will consistently assume Noble Intent, they will think more deeply about living up to your expectations. In other words, they will be motivated to have good reasons for behaving as they do.

Their behavior is influenced and modified in a positive manner. They are more inclined to explain their position, which will help the dialogue turn toward reaching an appreciation of the other person's outlook.

If people are going to adopt Noble Intent as a personal and professional value system, they must believe that others are motivated to do the right thing. What is right in their mind, of course, is based on that person's perspective, the information available to them, and their position in the world. So, it is possible for people to both assume Noble Intent and yet disagree with each other. How can that be? Doesn't someone have to be "right?" Can it actually be possible to respectfully disagree and understand their point of view? Could it be achievable to reach a compromise that involves two different views remaining respectfully opposed? Can the two parties agree to respectfully disagree? Is it all right to put together a workable solution that allows all parties to find the middle ground for the best of the organization? Often, viewing the issues from the Noble Intent vantage point is the best way to move forward.

"Every man, however good, has a yet better man within him. When the outer man is unfaithful to his deeper convictions, the hidden man whispers a protest. The name of this hidden whisper in the soul is conscience."

-Friedrich Heinrich Alexander Von Homboldt

Perceptual Prisms and Positions

When you assume Noble Intent, these are questions you should automatically ask before imposing judgment. Assuming Noble Intent should begin with understanding the other person's point of view before passing judgment or making your final decisions. In order to do this effectively, you must be familiar with the concept of perceptual prisms and perceptual positioning.

When you take in information, the messages from your senses - sight, sound, smell, intuition, touch and feelings - are filtered through your unique perceptual prism. This prism is made up of the delicate mix of your background, values, judgments, decisions, emotions, morals, and life experiences.

How we feel about or behave toward a situation, topic or idea is determined largely by how our prism has interpreted the sensory data we take in combined with our attitude, feelings about the situation, and temperament at any given moment. It's a given that each person's prism would be unique and different from anyone else's prism. Every thought or image that reaches your mind has been funneled, distorted, honed, and refined through your unique perceptual prism. So, while we may have experiences similar to other people, we still may react differently. Furthermore, how we react today may not be how we respond five years from now. Because we are constantly changing throughout life, our perceptual prism is continually adjusting to new input. It is steadily changing based on how we sort through new information and how we currently process that information. The beliefs we adhere to today are open to change as we learn and grow and experience more of life.

Thus, what you consider right based on your current perceptual prism may not match my understanding of what I believe is right, based on my current perceptual prism. The good news is that within perceptual prisms we have perceptual positions. Each person's perceptual prism can be viewed from three distinctly different perspectives. This is where understanding occurs. If I cannot change how I view a situation and still be able to hold my viewpoint, I will not be willing to look at the other point of view. Yet, if I can still keep my point of view and merely seek to understand yours, I will remain comfortable enough to remain open-minded. This allows for the possibility of initiating change. When that impasse is met, your job is to uncover the other person's motivation based on their Noble Intent so you might influence them to change the way they think or act.

On a larger scale, remember the last time someone cut you off in traffic? I'm guessing you had some choice words that included "stupid, jerk, etc." and every unprintable epithet you could spit out. Or maybe your boss told you he didn't like the way you were dressed. That was pretty darn rude, not to mention embarrassing. In the first case, it is doubtful that you will ever know why the driver cut you off. The poor fellow may have had an 18-wheeler breathing down his back. Or, he may have simply misjudged how fast you were going and inadvertently cut you off. In either case, had

"The man who is worthy of being a leader of men will never complain about the stupidity of his helpers, the ingratitude of mankind nor the in-appreciation of the public. These are all a part of the great game of life. To meet them and overcome them and not to go down before them in disgust, discouragement or defeat - that is the final proof of power."

-William J. H. Boetcker

you assumed Noble Intent you would not have reacted angrily while wasting energy and emotion over something you could not control.

The second instance actually happened to me many years ago. I always dress quite professionally in expensive, flattering, business suits. One day I had an appointment with a local supermarket manager. I had worked with another manager in the chain and noticed that everyone dressed rather casually. So I dressed casually. On the way to my appointment I stopped by the office. My boss happened by and stopped short when he saw me. He asked: "Hellen, do you have an appointment?" I said, "Yes, I do." Then he asked if I was going to the appointment dressed that way and I responded yes. That was the wrong answer.

He told me that clients - whether they are Fortune 500 executives or owner-operator businesses - expect people in our industry to dress professionally. It shows respect for the client and a professional attitude on our part. Then he directed me to go home and change.

Driving home I was absolutely furious. My boss had always complimented the way I dressed. I muttered and cursed him all the way home. I even considered quitting before I calmed down and realized that he was right. Had I been versed in the tenets of assuming Noble Intent I would have realized that my boss's comment was inconsistent with the way he normally acted. Consistent behavior is a bedrock of assuming Noble Intent. When someone acts out of the norm, there is always a reason. Your job is to find out why.

Had I assumed Noble Intent, I would have searched for the reason behind my boss's comment and realized that I had unwittingly crossed a line. He was merely helping me correct a mistake and help my career. From that point on I have always dressed in an upscale, professional manner. Even in today's more casual business world, I pride myself in presenting

"No one is my enemy, none a stranger and everyone is my friend."

-*Sikhism,* Guru Arjan Dev : AG 1299

an image that demands respect and attention. This lesson would not have been so painful had I known to assume Noble Intent immediately.

People are often unreasonable, illogical, and self-centered ~
Forgive them anyway.

If you are kind, people may accuse you of selfish, ulterior
motives ~ Be kind anyway.

If you are successful, you will win some false friends and
some true enemies ~ Succeed anyway.

If you are honest and frank, people may cheat you ~
Be honest and frank anyway.

What you spend years building, someone could destroy
overnight ~ Build anyway.

If you find serenity and happiness, they may be jealous ~
Be happy anyway.

The good you do today, people will often forget tomorrow ~
Do good anyway.

Give the world the best you have, and it may never be
enough ~ Give the world the best you've got anyway.

You see, in the final analysis, it is between you and God ~
It was never between you and them anyway.

Author: Mother Teresa

Chapter 15

Assuming Noble Intent at Work

On Average and Over Time Trust Loans are a great investment!

The day Willy Schweikert was introduced to the concept of assuming Noble Intent, he reacted the way most managers do - he rolled his eyes and thought, "Yeah, right, that's going to work. Too touchy-feely!"

Under the bravado, however, Schweikert was desperately searching for a way to improve his work environment. A corporate culture steeped in mistrust had already compelled him to transfer from his company's Southern California office to its Florida site. The stress in California had been so all consuming that his hair turned pre-maturely gray and he added 60 unneeded pounds.

"The whole California facility was a culture of do what you have to do for yourself and do not trust the people around you," he said.

To his dismay, Schweikert discovered that the only thing his cross-country move had changed was the ocean he looked out on. His new Florida work environment had the same bickering, distrust, and me-first attitude.

That first night after we talked, Schweikert went home and thought about what assuming Noble Intent required. Lying in bed, he decided to give it a try. He would consciously choose to believe that people wanted to do the right thing, including the two employee agent provocateurs he was sure were out to get him fired. He would find out what was motivating their behavior and go from there. He started the next day with a new philosophy of assuming Noble Intent.

A year later Schweikert could be the poster boy for assuming Noble Intent. His hair is still gray, but he has shed 53 pounds and is happy again. Assuming Noble Intent has completely changed his relationship with his peers, employees, and even his family members.

"Once you assume Noble Intent there is a lot more trust," he said. "You know there is no overt political agenda to make you lose your job. From an organizational standpoint we know that we are all trying to get to the same place. It has built a very close top-level organization. We trust each other and communicate with each other."

While assuming Noble Intent has not spread like wild fire with his staff, Schweikert does see a difference. For instance, the long line of people waiting at his door to complain and whine has disappeared. People are now working together as a team, not as individuals with personal agendas.

"From an overall organization we are much more aligned to a common goal and not nearly as fragmented as when I got here," he said. "It's a cohesive working organization. The team is working closer together now."

Assuming Noble Intent was a "leap of faith" for Schweikert and is something he still has to con-

> "It is never a question with any of us of faith or no faith; the question always is, 'In what or in whom do we put our faith?'"
>
> -Anonymous

> "Man may doubt here and there, but mankind does not doubt. The universal conscience is larger than the individual conscience, and that constantly comes in to correct and check our own infidelity."
>
> -Hugh Reginald Haweis: Speech in Season, Bk. III, 328

> "There are three acts of faith; assent, acceptance, and assurance."
>
> -John Flavel

sciously think about it. Habitually, he preaches the concept at every meeting. Predictably, he gets the same eye-rolling, you've-got-to-be-kidding-me expressions he once gave. It does not matter because he knows it works for him.

"Assuming Noble Intent has become sort of an evangelical thing with me," he said. "It is a journey and it will continue to be a journey. Life feels better. I've got an attitude that people are not trying to put me in the grave. People have good hearts. They just have to adjust their behavior."

Even though assuming Noble Intent is still a work in progress for Schweikert, his team is already enjoying the benefits that accompany the value system. For example, they have gone from a culture of mistrust to one of understanding and awareness. Reactionary, adversarial behavior and conflicts have dropped significantly. People are working together, which means silos and hierarchical barriers have fallen. Noble Intent has been a catalyst for multi-dimensional transformation inside Schweikert's organization.

Before Schweikert can spread the Noble Intent value system to more people inside his department and beyond, it will need to become second nature to him. He must fully understand why people surrender an old belief for a new and different one. He must understand the theory of cognitive dissonance.

Cognitive dissonance is a primary motivator for attitude and behavioral changes in people. Cognition is thinking, and thinking leads to our judgments of fact and fiction. This is filtered through our perceptual prism. Dissonance is a feeling of dissension, disagreement, conflict, discord, or a difference of opinion with what you thought was a fact. This cognitive dissonance can be based on your perception of what is occurring, versus what you thought should be happening. It could be just a feeling you get when you think about a person's actions or it could be based on consistent behavior you are observing. When a perception, action or behavior does not match what we believe should occur, this causes cognitive dissonance. This is most often felt as a disconnection or inconsistency among certain cognitions - that we acquire knowledge through using reasoning, by intuition or through our perception of the situation.

For instance, if a person is expecting you to react in a particular way, but instead you assume Noble Intent, the person's cognition - what they believe you are going to do - is thrown out of kilter. Because we humans do not like inconsistency in our beliefs and opinions, we try to fix the dissonance. That sometimes requires us to change our position. Whether or not we make the change depends on the amount and strength of the dissonance. The more important and dramatic the dissonance, the more likely we will adjust our beliefs.

Assuming a person is acting with Noble Intent essentially communicates an expectation. Even if this expectation is not accurate, people will act in ways that are consistent with the expectation. Thus the expectation is met and the person acts with Noble Intent even if the assumption of Noble Intent was false. In essence, the assumption of Noble Intent in many cases creates a self-fulfilling prophecy and a demonstration of the Pygmalion effect. In short, if you want people to act with Noble Intent, you must first assume that they are acting with Noble Intent or will act with Noble Intent given that expectation exists.

"In life we shall find many men that are great, and some who are good, but very few men are both great and good."

-Charles Caleb Colton

Expectations Can Frame How Citizens Behave

In 1993, the leadership of South Africa was faced with the daunting task of reconciling the past with the present. The country's leaders realized that their constituents' expectations must be evaluated and reconciled in order to rekindle hope and build a strong country and a new democracy from the ashes of apartheid. How best to accomplish this? This was the dilemma. Leaders recognized that the path forward was going to be difficult without bringing together the citizens to talk about the past. They asked: How to do this with a view of healing wounds? They formed the South African Truth and Reconciliation Commission for this purpose. The following is a section of the South African Constitution entitled *National Unity and Reconciliation*. Read the words and understand how this document provided the expectation of proceeding with the Principles of Noble Intent.

"A person with ubuntu is open and available to others, affirming of others, does not feel threatened that others are able and good, for he or she has a proper self-assurance that comes from knowing that he or she belongs in a greater whole and is diminished when others are humiliated or diminished, when others are tortured or oppressed."

-Archbishop Desmond Tutu

This Constitution provides a historic bridge between the past of a deeply divided society characterised by strife, conflict, untold suffering and injustice, and a future founded on the recognition of human rights, democracy and peaceful co-existence and development opportunities for all South Africans, irrespective of colour, race, class, belief or sex.

The pursuit of national unity, the well-being of all South African citizens and peace require

reconciliation between the people of South Africa and the recon-
struction of society.

The adoption of this Constitution lays the secure foundation for the
people of South Africa to transcend the divisions and strife of the
past, which generated gross violations of human rights, the trans-
gression of humanitarian principles in violent conflicts and a legacy
of hatred, fear, guilt and revenge.

These can now be addressed on the basis that there is a need for un-
derstanding but not for vengeance, a need for reparation but not for
retaliation, a need for ubuntu[3] but not for victimisation.

In order to advance such reconciliation and reconstruction, amnesty
shall be granted in respect of acts, omissions and offences associated
with political objectives and committed in the course of the conflicts
of the past. To this end, Parliament under this Constitution shall
adopt a law determining a firm cut-off date, which shall be a date
after 8 October 1990 and before 6 December 1993, and providing for
the mechanisms, criteria and procedures, including tribunals, if any,
through which such amnesty shall be dealt with at any time after the
law has been passed.

With this Constitution and these commitments we, the people of
South Africa, open a new chapter in the history of our country[4].

Nkosi sikelel' iAfrika. God seen Suid-Afrika. Morena boloka sechaba
sa heso. May God bless our country. Mudzimu fhatutshedza Afrika.
Hosi katekisa Afrika.

Nelson Mandela explained Ubuntu in this way:

A traveler through our country would stop at a village, and he didn't
have to ask for food or for water. Once he stops, the people give him
food, entertain him. That is one aspect of Ubuntu but it'll have various
aspects. Ubuntu does not mean that people should not enrich themselves. The question therefore is: Are you going to do so in order to
enable the community around you to improve?

---

3 Ubuntu is a South African ethic or ideology stemming from a Zulu and Xhola
word that encompasses a wide range of positive connotations from 'forgiveness'
to 'solidarity' and 'love for our fellow man'. Ubuntu focuses on people's
allegiances and relations with each other. It embraces humanity towards others
and the belief in a universal bond of sharing that connects all humanity. It is
widely used in South African English. In an African context, Ubuntu suggests
that the person is to become by behaving with humanity is an ancestor worthy
of respect or admiration. Those who uphold the principle of ubuntu throughout
their lives will, in death, achieve a unity with those still living.
4 Other nations have followed South Africa's example and used this as a basis
for their commissions.

Chapter 16

Reconciling Cognitive Dissonance

Cognitive dissonance often occurs in our daily lives in something as simple as a purchase we make. Imagine that you bought a car and shortly afterward you had doubts about your choice. For starters, you never really cared for dark colored cars. Yet, you purchased a hybrid car in a dark color. At first you liked the car well-enough and you grew accustomed to the color, but the fact is whenever you drove it, you still yearned for a little more power and comfort. Consequently, you are now suffering from the stress of cognitive dissonance.

To eliminate the dissonance, you have to rationalize your buying decision to feel comfortable that it was a choice you would make again. How do you do this? Well, you can tell yourself that more power is not as important as saving energy. As for the color, even though you still prefer lighter colored cars, you can offset that dissonance by reminding yourself that you saved hundreds of dollars by buying the car straight off the lot. Finally, having driven the car for a few months, you realize for longer drives, the car simply is not very comfortable. With this you can again remind yourself that your terrific fuel savings overrides your discomfort. Or you can simply take this experience as a lesson learned and say to yourself: "There is nothing much I can do about it today. I choose to ignore it. Although, the next time I go car shopping, I'll rent one for a few days first. This was a good lesson in car buying."

Now, let's look at the process of resolving cognitive dissonance. You came to terms with this type of purchase through a series of steps. To balance your purchase with your beliefs, you immediately compared and contrasted the importance of the difference -- horsepower versus the energy saving aspects of the hybrid. To counter balance another dissonance - color - you added more consonant beliefs – initial price and cost savings through great gas mileage. Finally, you brought your remaining dissonant beliefs - uncomfortable on long road trips - into line by simply changing them. Tip: To minimize cognitive dissonance or completely avoid it, we recommend you write a list of features/traits/criteria you desire in a major event (car purchase, home purchase, job change, life partner, etc.). The less you deviate from your list, the less cognitive dissonance you will experience.

Resolving cognitive dissonance is more problematic when the two alternatives are equally attractive. This often happens in the decision making process in large corporations. Usually what happens is a decision is made and goes forward. Before long, however, some unforeseen negative aspects arise. People begin to second-guess the decision - cognitive dissonance - because in reality the decision is not unfolding as flawlessly as expected. To offset cognitive dissonance, they ask to revisit the decision making process. The best way to reduce the dissonance is by addressing possible consequences of the decision more thoroughly during the decision-making process.

At the department level, assuming Noble Intent and cognitive dissonance work hand in glove. One person assuming Noble Intent often triggers cognitive dissonance in the other person that must be resolved. In his article, "The Benefit of the Doubt," Roy D. Follendore, III points out that doubts change our belief system.

"Like pain, doubt protects us from both ourselves as well as external threats," Follendore writes. "Without pain we would continue to touch hot surfaces and would often never know when we are sick, injured or threatened. Doubt does for our philosophical systems what pain does for our physical system. Doubt allows us the flexibility to change our orientations in ways that protect us by signaling to our rational minds that our philosophy may be inappropriate."

In Follendore's article, assuming Noble Intent and reconciling doubt can be seen as two sides of the same coin. By assuming Noble Intent, the person is reconciling a doubt. They may be unsure of the other person's intentions but are willing to grant them the benefit of the doubt. The second person, in turn, observes behavior that may be inconsistent with their intentions. Since the reaction is unanticipated, cognitive dissonance results.

In the real world it may play out something like this. We all know that a person's mark of power inside a company relates to the number of people and size of the budget under their control. Now take two managers - Mary and Sam - who are peers in a highly competitive and confrontational situation. For business reasons the company has decided to shift resources and people away from Sam and allocate them to Mary.

Stung by the loss of influence, Sam may believe that Mary and her executive friends have been plotting against him because they want a woman in a high-profile position. To get even he could poison the people he is losing by telling them Mary is a terrible manager, or in some other way resist the change.

An alternative response is for Sam to assume Noble Intent. He might realize that the company's direction or Mary's talent and not her chromosome count were the deciding factors. He may also assume that the move is for the greater good of the company. In either case, Sam would tell his departing employees that, while he hated losing them, this was a good, solid business decision and that Mary is a wonderful manager.

A third possibility exists. Mary, realizing that Sam's ego has taken a hit, may reach out to him. She could tell Sam that she's sorry if he feels badly about how things have worked out for him but that they are both working for the same goal and if the corporation thrives, they will both benefit. Mary's reaching out and acting with Noble Intent will cause a grumpy Sam to have cognitive dissonance.

In the scenario where Sam believes people are plotting against him, he has no dissonance because his perception of reality matches his beliefs. But when Mary approaches him and acts with Noble Intent, it shatters that harmony.

He now has doubts. Did this all happen because Mary was in cahoots with the big-wigs or is it a genuinely solid business decision based on what is best for the company, and ultimately him? His choice is to reconcile that doubt with one of two options: The corporation and Mary are acting with Noble Intent or not.

What happens when people do not act with or assume Noble Intent? There is no better way to illustrate the results when Noble Intent is missing than the story of Stanislav Petrov. For years during the Cold War, neither the United States nor the Soviet Union acted with or assumed Noble Intent. Instead they pointed untold numbers of nuclear tipped missiles at each other. Both sides kept a wary eye on the other, monitoring each other's missile sites for the slightest hint of a pre-emptive attack. At the first sign of a launch, the other was prepared to retaliate and most likely destroy the world.

Into this cauldron walked Petrov, a lieutenant colonel in the former Soviet Union Army. Petrov was on duty the night of September 26, 1983. His job was to monitor the early warning computers and satellites that would detect a missile attack from the United States. It was just after

"You can't escape the responsibility of tomorrow by evading it today."

-Abraham Lincoln

"People can be such jerks. Other people. Not you and me. When we get upset and are impatient or short with people, it's for good and valid reasons. If people could only see the pressures we're under or the unfairness of the situations we have to deal with."

-Dan Coulter

midnight in the Soviet Union - still mid-afternoon of the previous day in the United States. Suddenly an alarm started blaring indicating that a missile had been launched from the United States heading on course for the Soviet Union. Fortunately, Petrov thought it did not make sense that the United States would launch just one missile. No, he reasoned, if the United States was going to launch an attack it would be an all-out attack. He decided it was a computer glitch and ignored the warning.

A short time later the computer warnings started sounding again. This time it showed multiple missiles - as many as five - incoming. With the warning sirens wailing he stared nervously at his console and the flashing "start launch" button that would commence a massive counter attack in front of him, Petrov had a difficult decision to make. His training told him he should initiate the launch codes immediately, but he had a pervasive feeling that this second warning was also a computer error. Still, he could not know for sure. He had only minutes to decide what he should tell the Soviet leadership. His career, his life and his country were at stake with his pending decision.

He chose to trust his intuition. He declared the missile alert a false alarm and then he sat back - hyperventilating - and waited. Seconds rolled into minutes. Nothing happened, no explosions. In fact, everything was quiet. He had made the right decision. He kept the earth from becoming an irradiated cinder. He was a hero. Predictably, instead of being treated like a hero, Petrov's superiors questioned him intensely for disobeying military procedure. He was not punished, but his military career was over. He was transferred to a less sensitive position and two years later retired from the service.

Petrov saved the world because he chose to assume that the United States was acting with Noble Intent, which was a career-ending decision. You must remember that in 1983 the Cold War and the tension between the two countries were at an all-time high. Gratefully, one man did what two nations could not bring themselves to do - give the other the benefit of the doubt. In doing so, that one man saved the world.

Playing devil's advocate: If we stop and think about this example from different perspectives, did Petrov truly act with Noble Intent? From his superiors' point of view, the answer would be different from the American public's standpoint. Can there be more than one way of looking at Noble Intent? Our conclusion: Noble Intent is based on the personal perspective of the one acting with Noble Intent. Noble Intent is subjective but must be based on what most cultures would agree to be the right thing to do. Our task is to understand the other person's view of Noble Intent if it differs from what we expected.

Almost sixty years earlier, people were hoping that the last global war had been fought. World War I was supposed to be the war to end all wars. In his 1926 presentation speech at the No-bel Award Ceremony, Fridtjof Nansen, the Peace Laureate for 1922, talked about how the United States, acting with Noble Intent, had helped Europe back on its feet and convinced the other allies to reduce the amount of Germany's reparations. Acting with Noble Intent, Nansen said, had also changed the psychology in Europe and opened the door to reconciliation. Other agreements would follow to ensure nations would no longer pick up arms against each other. Nansen warned that those nations had to transform all those good words and thoughts into actions.

"Noble words and Noble Intent on the part of leaders are a great encouragement, but they are not enough," he said. "Words must be translated into action, intent into earnest toil, for shining promises have often come to nothing in the past and the blue skies of hope have again been filled by storm clouds."

Try as they might, the words of Noble Intent never made the transition into actions of Noble Intent. Nine years after his speech, the storm clouds of war again began forming over Europe. There would be yet another war to end all wars. Acting with and assuming Noble Intent only works when the words are connected to a deeper, personal value system that is committed to action.

"Never attribute to malice that which can be adequately explained by stupidity."

- Hanlon's Razor

Chapter 17

Decision Making with Noble Intent

Noble Leadership is about acting with and assuming Noble Intent. Noble Leadership is about listening to people - to those who agree and those that disagree with you - and making fair and honest decisions that work for the people and the enterprise. That's because Noble Leadership is about doing the right thing each time, every time.

Noble Leadership is defined more by the way decisions are reached and the values underpinning the decision-making process than the actual decision itself. In the end, if you have Noble Intent as the underpinning for your decision-making processes, your employees will do their best to make each decision succeed, even those they disagree with.

"It is a great mistake to think of being great without goodness; and I pronounce it is certain that there was never yet a truly great man that was not at the same time truly virtuous."

-Benjamin Franklin

The boss's goals aren't the only agenda items at this meeting!

The best way to develop the kind of decision-making process employees can get behind is to first build a reputation as a Noble Leader - a leader who practices and assumes Noble Intent. Once you have established your Noble Intent credentials, the rest is a matter of following through. For instance, a good decision-making process should be as transparent as glass. It should address problems through open discussions and honest deliberations. It should allow people to have their voices heard, even when you know that what they have to say will not change the decision.

"Life is made up of little things. It is very rarely that an occasion is offered for doing a great deal at once. True greatness consists in being great in the little thing."

-Charles Simmons

President Franklin D. Roosevelt employed Noble Leadership better than most. According to Erwin C. Hargrove's The President as Leader, Roosevelt enjoyed letting his advisors fight through contradictory courses of action in meetings. He would listen to both sides before developing a solution that would consider all viewpoints.

An effective Noble Leader must influence people to do what they want, when they want, and how they want it done. A naturally sunny disposition and charming personality is a plus for a leader. Frankly, it is not necessary. An effective leader does need something they can trade, exchange, or give to influence people in a positive way. I am not talking about bribes, at least not literally. But it is a kind of a quid pro quo - you do something I want, I will give you something you want in return. That currency - trust, respect and confidence - is the oil that greases the decision-making process. You have earned it as the leader and can spend it to ensure that your decisions succeed.

Before we get into why building an effective decision making process is important, let us first discuss leaders and their three different kinds of currency: (1) positional power, 2) personal power and 3) hybrid personal/positional power. There is raw, positional power, what I like to call the "It is good to be the king," power, or in the case of the United States, "It is good to be the president." The power is embedded in the job. Then there is personal power, the kind that you either earn or is given to you by the people you lead because they trust, respect, and admire you. Again, Roosevelt's use of personal power stands out.

"He drew strength for leadership from empathy and connections established with others, both individuals and large audiences," Hargrove writes. "He used his charm to dominate and, at the same time, to inspire and encourage others to act in his service... He knew how to weave a web of action from competing advisors, in public appeals, and in feeling his way toward politically viable legislation."

Finally,there is a hybrid of personal and positional power - a sort of carrot-and-stick approach. The mere knowledge that you possess a stick, even if you have never used it, is in itself a powerful motivator.

Clearly, positional power is the easiest of the three to wield. You simply order people to do what you want or the stick comes out. It has next to nothing to do with exercising Noble Intent or earning trust, respect and confidence. Your employees will likely grumble about you behind your back. You really do not want to use positional power alone. It is not an effective long-term way to run a corporation or a department. You want people on board with your decisions, not thinking of ways to sabotage them. Remember, people who act out of fear are not invested in your mission and do not act or assume Noble Intent. The best leaders rarely overtly use their positional power.

The most satisfying leadership currency to spend is personal power. It is an amazing feeling when your team is pulling together out of trust and respect for you. It is not necessary to have any positional power for your personal power to be effective. You can accomplish an incredible amount using just personal power. Take Candy Lightner, for example. You may not recognize her name, but she is the founder of Mothers Against Drunk Driving (MADD). After a drunken driver killed her 13-year-old daughter, Lightner began a campaign to change drinking and driving laws.

"Those who enjoy responsibility usually get it; those who merely like exercising authority usually lose it."

Malcolm Forbes

Through activism and strong leadership based in Noble Intent, Lightner, a Realtor by profession, not only influenced changes in the law, but altered how we view drinking and driving. Today there are MADD chapters throughout the United States and in every English-speaking country in the world. Lightner did it all with the personal power she earned because people trusted and respected her. They believed her crusade was based in Noble Intent.

The hybrid personal/positional power is probably the most practical leadership currency. While a leader can go far using just personal power, it never hurts to have the muscle to leverage positional power. Remember, as a leader you ultimately have the final decision-making authority. If people cannot reach agreement, or are running out of time, the decision falls to you. When you unveil your decision, make sure it is supported by a solid rationale. Yes, you are using raw positional power, although it is not precipitous and it is for the good of the company and everyone involved.

We know the source of positional power. Yet, how exactly do you accrue personal power? Start with Noble Intent. If Noble Intent is your personal value system it means you don't tell lies, cheat, or tell half-truths. It also means you are up-front and honest with people. If your employees know that you practice Noble Intent, they are secure in assuming that you will act with Noble Intent toward them. When you act and assume Noble Intent, you earn their trust and respect. The cycle will continue as long as you hold up your end of the bargain - that is, practicing Noble Intent.

Once again, Roosevelt is a prime example of a leader who was honest and forthright with his constituents. Hargrove writes that Roosevelt "Believed that if people understood the facts, if they understood the reasons behind a government action or policy, if they were taken into the confidence of their government and received a full and truthful statement of what was happen-

"True greatness is the most ready to recognize and most willing to obey those simple outward laws which have been sanctioned by the experience of mankind."

-J. A. Froude

ing, they would generally choose the right course. He also felt it was part of his job of leadership to give them those facts. There lay the greatest source of the President's strength. He was able to explain to the people the most intricate problems of government. He could do it by the use of simple language and by the clear, confident, and persuasive tone of his voice."

What happens when you act with Noble Intent but something goes wrong? For instance, you make a promise that, for whatever reason, you cannot deliver. Following through on promises is vital. But not every promise can be kept. When you cannot keep a promise, go back to basics. Be upfront with people and tell the truth. Explain the whole truth, without embellishment. Tell people why you had to alter the decision. Explain how going forward with the previous decision would hurt them and the company. Take them through why you thought reversing the decision was in the best interests of the constituents. If you are effective at communicating this, even though you have to break a promise, you will still be seen as acting with Noble Intent.

How do you build a good decision making process? First of all, the list of reasons for creating one is longer than the grocery list for a family with teenagers. If you ask any leader if they have the necessary data to make an informed decision about a particular problem they most likely will say yes. In reality, they often don't. As a leader you have to make sure that your decision-making process is solid and that everyone in your organization understands how decision-making processes affect long-term results. Remember the Domino Effect. Nowhere is it more important than in decision-making and alignment. Decisions are the core of actions and actions are the building blocks of results. Good decisions based on Noble Intent will bring good results based on Principles of Noble Intent.

Jim Torgerson has managed the best of people, he has managed the worst of people. In fact, veteran corporate executive Jim Torgerson, president and chief executive officer of UIL Holdings, has successfully managed a myriad of personalities guided by one business philosophy: Noble Intent.

"I believe people are basically good and want to do the right thing," said Torgerson. "I am willing to work with them and bring those attributes out."

Experience has taught Torgerson that the surest way to draw out those attributes is by giving people a voice in the decision-making process. Inviting different perspectives and ideas adds to the richness of the discussion and decision-making process.

"You want different thinking," Torgerson said. "I don't have all the answers. You rely on other people for input." But perhaps more important, giving people a seat at the table personally invests them in the project. And that makes them more likely to support whatever decision is reached. Torgerson has found that those who vigorously disagree with him during discussions are often the staunchest supporters of the final decision.

"Most people, as long as they get a fair hearing and an explanation, may not like it but they will move on," he said. "If you just say, this is the direction but not say why, it's hard to get alignment."

Without alignment, a project cannot succeed. Think of it this way: Every upper-level management decision is like arranging dominoes. To make the dominoes topple uniformly, each tile must be aligned precisely, beginning with the first. If just one tile is out of alignment, the cascade will abruptly stop, leaving the remaining pieces standing.

In business, the first dominoes are the CEO and board. Their decision radiates out to managers who send the message down through the organization's ranks. If everyone is properly aligned, the decision is successfully implemented. But if a board member, manager or team leader simply does nothing to support the decision, the policy or project will almost certainly fail.

"To believe all men honest would be folly. To believe none so, is something worse."

-John Quincy Adams

"The price of greatness is responsibility."

-Winston Churchill

"The question 'Who ought to be boss?' is like asking 'Who ought to be the tenor in the quartet?' Obviously, the man who can sing tenor."

-Henry Ford

# Chapter 18
Communicating with Noble Intent

With this loan, we trust you will do the right thing

Every day you tell the world who you are and what you stand for by what you say and what you do. Old sayings like, "Your word is your bond," and "Actions speak louder than words," still hold meaning today because they define character in simple, direct terms.

Character springs from a value system that encourages the right choices. Those choices are based on what we think about a situation from information filtered through our unique perceptual prisms. Consequently, some of our thoughts are good, while others are not. Sometimes, the difference between the two is all but indiscernible and utterly confusing. Remember as a child watching cartoons where a character facing a tough choice has a good angel appear on one shoulder whispering advice, while on the other a pitch-forked devil character is doing the same thing. What separates us as people are the thoughts we choose to embrace. Your collection of daily decisions will ultimately create the legacy of your life.

Choosing wisely requires that you first check your perception. Be sure that you are acting on correct information. Quiz yourself about the situation. Is everything as it appears? Does another possible explanation exist? Is what the person saying out of character? Have I failed to account for something?

Remember David Pelzer, the author whose mother dehumanized him by stripping away his name and calling him "It"? Pelzer could have easily, and understandably, succumbed to the devil whispering on his shoulder. Instead, he listened to the angel and utilized positive self-talk to survive those horrible years. Today, David is a productive, contributing member of society.

The top performers in every field will tell you that self-talk helps you process information and work toward a decision. It also reduces stress by forcing your mind to analyze the situation in a cool, collected manner. Perhaps most important, self-talk allows you to transcend the basic questions which lead to fresh insights, innovative ideas, and new options. Finally, self-talk conditions your mind to make carefully considered decisions and better choices.

While self-talk relies on good information, it also banks on your word being your bond (noble)

"It doesn't take great men to do things, but it is doing things that make men great."

-Arnold Glasgow

and your actions speaking louder than words (intent). Said another way, self-talk depends on you having Noble Intent.

History is replete with incidents where words were bent to serve an agenda or promote a cause. The fact is, no word, no matter how precise its dictionary definition, is immune to the written or spoken alchemy of politicians, lawyers, radio talk show hosts, and yes, writers. Even its context within a sentence can twist a word's traditional meaning. United States Supreme Court Justice Oliver Wendell Holmes, Jr. understood all too well how words could be cleverly compromised to fit a specific situation or support a particular argument. Justice Holmes, himself a wordsmith known for crafting succinct, quotable opinions, once said, "A word is not a crystal, transparent and unchanged; it is the skin of a living thought, and may vary greatly in color and content according to the circumstances and time in which it is used."

As a manager living with Noble Intent, you will have to supervise your share of rule-benders. How do you get them to act and assume Noble Intent at work? The answer is surprisingly straight-forward. As a manager you cannot tell an employee how to conduct his/her private life. Fortunately, you most certainly can tell them what you expect from them while at work. Also, assume Noble Intent when communicating about the principle. Perhaps they were rule-benders because of their prior environment.

Have a conversation with every new person you hire, inherit or who transfers into your department. Explain to each person as clearly and plainly as possible how you expect them to behave. The conversation might go something like this: "Joe, I would like to welcome you to our team. I think you will find your colleagues are a great group of people. What makes this department such a pleasant place to work is that we treat each other with trust, respect and honesty. We call the principle that we adhere to Noble Intent. It is about believing that everyone is try-

"When a fellow thinks he is putting it over on the boss, the boss is not thinking of putting him over others to boss."

-C.K. Anderson

ing to do the right thing for the organization. We give our colleagues in the department, and the company at large, the benefit of the doubt. Noble Intent is part of our department's culture, our value system, and we expect everyone to respect that. Also, we all have agreed to act within the tenets of Noble Intent."

Explain to Joe the benefits of adopting Noble Intent in the office. In any event, your conversation has put Joe on notice. As Noble Intent is almost always a work in progress, it may take Joe some time to adapt. If he does not show Noble Intent at a meeting, privately bring it to his attention. Remind him again how you do business and what you expect from him. Make it abundantly clear that there are consequences if he continues to be rude, unkind or underhanded - "un-noble" as it were.

If Joe still refuses to incorporate Noble Intent at work, it is time for another heart-to-heart, followed by consequences. Before you mete out the punishment, check your own perception. Make sure you are on target.

"Joe, we have talked about your conduct in meetings before. How you talk to and treat people outside this company is your business. I told you from the beginning what I expect. You are either unable or unwilling to comply. I am going to have to log a formal report and speak to your boss for being disrespectful in our team meetings and less than truthful."

It is clear that Joe must shift his work value system to align with Noble Intent or leave the department and possibly the company. You can help him understand the need to change by asking two most poignant questions: What kind of person is he, and how does he want to be remembered? Does he want to be despised, distrusted and reviled in life, and ignored in death? Those two powerful questions usually stop the most cynical person in their tracks. After all, our legacy is all that remains after we have gone.

The surest path for Joe and anyone else who

"A good man likes a hard boss. I don't mean a nagging boss or a grouchy boss. I mean a boss who insists on things being done right and on time; a boss who is watching things closely enough so that he knows a good job from a poor one. Nothing is more discouraging to a good man than a boss who is not on the job, and who does not know whether things are going well or badly."

-William Feather

seeks a proud legacy is to adopt a Noble Intent value system. I believe that Noble Intent is already engrained in an overwhelming majority of corporate executives, department heads and managers. Unfortunately, it is hidden under years of bad leadership; like a fine piece of wood whose beautiful patina is concealed by layers and layers of paint. Scrape away the residue and remember how good it feels to do the right thing for the right reason. Ask yourself, "What is my Noble Intent? What are the things I can do to show Noble Intent? What are the things I say and do - that when I think about it - make me say, that is not me. I am not like that. I will not do that again."

Even so, acting with and assuming Noble Intent requires nurturing and vigilance. You will have to constantly check your values. A year after he adopted Noble Intent, Willy Schweikert still has to consciously think about Noble Intent. Every time you decide something ask yourself, "Is this the right thing to do? Am I being fair? Is what I am doing for the greater good of the company? Will I feel good about what I am doing later? Are my intentions pure? Am I compromising my values? Can I live with the consequences, both short and long term?"

Those questions will eventually become the tenants upon which your Noble Intent will rest.

But even then leading your people to act with Noble Intent is not a given. Take, for example, President Woodrow Wilson. In 1918, President Wilson delivered his famous Fourteen Points speech to a joint session of Congress 10 months before the end of the war. Throughout the speech, the president made it clear that the United States acted with Noble Intent when it entered the war.

"What we demanded in this war, therefore, is nothing peculiar to ourselves," he said. "It is that the world be made fit and safe to live in; particularly that it be made safe for every peace-loving nation which, like our own, wishes to live its own life, determine its own institutions, be assured of justice and fair dealing by the other peoples of the world as against force and selfish aggression."

At the conclusion of the speech, Wilson again made it clear that the United States would act with Noble Intent toward Germany once it surrendered.

"We have no jealousy of German greatness, and there is nothing in this program (the Fourteen Points) that impairs it," he concluded. "We grudge her no achievement or distinction of learning or of pacific enterprise such as have made her record very bright and very enviable. We do not wish to injure her or to block in any way her legitimate influence or power. We do not wish to fight her either with arms or with hostile arrangements of trade if she is willing to associate herself with us and the other peace-loving nations of the world in covenants of justice and law and fair dealing."

The speech became the framework for the German surrender and gave Wilson tremendous moral standing in the world. But try as he might to make the United States a world leader, Congress refused to sign the 1919 Treaty of Versailles. Nor could he convince Congress to join the new League of Nations, an institution he believed would prevent wars by acting with Noble Intent. At one point in another speech to Congress, he asked what was stopping the legislative body from acting with Noble Intent.

"Now, what is the trouble?" he asked. "What are they afraid of? I want you to put this to every man you know who makes this objection - what is he afraid of?"

"The golden rule should apply as much to spirit of doing business as to spirituality.

Hurt not others in ways that you yourself would find hurtful."

Buddhism, Udana-Varga 5:18

Chapter 19

Communicating Your
Noble Intent to Others

Sometimes, you will be faced with the fact that others will be against what you are trying to achieve. When this happens, you must be able to communicate your view of your Noble Intent principles succinctly. You must put forth an argument that explains why your views have merit - even when faced with seemingly insurmountable obstacles.

Thomas Jefferson spent several months dialoging with the British in an attempt to get them to understand the Colonies' Noble Intent - to be treated fairly and be given a modicum of self-determination. His words were meant to avert war and change the balance of power, in order to create a symbiotic relationship for the good of all. As we know, his message (below) fell on deaf ears. Even though he knew there was little chance of success, he still did the right thing and behaved with Noble Intent.

Fortunately, most of the time in organizations, you will find less resistance to Noble Intent. If communicated clearly, Noble Intent will frequently prevail.

"These, my lord, are our sentiments, on this important subject, which we offer only as an individual part of the whole empire. Final determination we leave to the general congress, now sitting, before whom we shall lay the papers your lordship has communicated to us. For ourselves, we have exhausted every mode of application, which our invention could suggest, as proper and promising. We have decently remonstrated with parliament—they have added new injuries to the old; we have wearied our king with supplications—he has not deigned to answer us; we have appealed to the native honour and justice of the British nation—their efforts in our favour have hitherto been ineffectual. What then remains to be done? That we commit our injuries to the even handed justice of that Being, who doth no wrong, earnestly beseeching Him to illuminate the councils, and prosper the endeavours of those to whom America hath confided her hopes; that through their wise directions, we may again see reunited the blessings of liberty, prosperity, and harmony with Great Britain."

-Thomas Jefferson, written in 1775 as a plea for fairness from Great Britain in their dealings with the American Colonies prior to the signing of the Declaration of Independence.

Some business leaders prefer painting their decisions in shades of gray. They like the maneuverability that subtly and nuance afford them.

Not Thomas Jefferson, not Jim White. When it comes to running a business and communicating Noble Intent, the chief operating officer of J.L. International works in two colors - black and white. And for White that means you either practice and communicate with Noble Intent, or you work for another company.

"I have been singing the (Noble Intent) song for almost 40 years," White said. "I am the person who has been pushing the (Noble Intent) envelope in corporate American way before it became sexy."

Noble Intent was anything but sexy when White was first introduced to the concept. He was only eight-years-old when his grandfather taught him what it takes to be a good person and an honest human being.

"He was a great mentor and a teacher," White said of his grandfather. "His words were simple but very profound for me. He told me, 'You must do what you say you are going to do, and those actions must be with the utmost integrity.' Those words, as a kid, I do not know why, they stuck with me."

Those words became an integral part of White's value system and beliefs. He has carried them into every company he has worked for or owned. Over the years he has pared the message down to a series of bullet points on a single sheet of paper. Every employee understands White's vision for the company and what they can and cannot do to fulfill that vision.

"If you are not going to align with that, you are not welcomed to be part of our family," said White, who has bought and sold twenty-two companies. "We are talking about values and Noble Intent, what we stand for and making sure we get the right people in the right boat, going in the right direction."

More than once, White has had to fire employees who have chosen to ignore his business values. In one case, White was hired to run a company that had one employee responsible for sixty percent of a department's profits. But White did not like the employee's money-making methods or morals.

"He was slick and smooth and he had the personality," he said. "But every behavior was cutting corners here or cheating on the expense account report, or putting language in the contract that you know is going to cause problems for the client organization. It was just the stuff you had to stay up at night trying to figure out how to do it wrong."

White's bosses were less concerned about the salesman's style as long as he kept bringing in the cash. As long as they had plausible deniability and the employee did not cause them to be dragged into court, everything was fine. So when White announced that he was going to cut the money-maker loose, they were not happy. But he did it anyway.

"I called the individual in and said, give me your credit card and keys," White said. "You are fired."

White informed the rest of the sales team, telling them that he fired the No. 1 money-maker because it was in the best interest of the team, the company and its clients. He said the team was not only going to meet its quarterly goal, but he expected them to exceed the numbers - and to do it with integrity. To his surprise, team members were overjoyed. They told White they were glad that someone had finally done something about the salesman. And just as White had predicted, the team did exceed its goal. People who had been 'B' players stepped up their game to the 'A' level.

"It was like removing a black cloud," he said. "Everyone laughed again and cooperated with each other. It became fun and business came without forcing it. This value base is absolutely critical to us but we are going to make good money while doing it. I do not believe that you have to throw all your morals out the door to do that."

White believes that most people start out with Noble Intent and want to do a good job. But for various reasons, they drift and forget about Noble Intent along the way.

"If you come from a background with little money and you start making more than you thought and you get a taste of the good life, you could start sliding a little bit," he said.

White is always willing to give people the benefit of the doubt. That is why every employee is given that single sheet of paper with the company's values and vision. It is what the company stands for and will die for. It is the employee's responsibility not to violate those principles.

"There are no second chances, no questions asked," White said about people who ignore Noble Intent. "You cannot continue to build an organization that becomes solid, with a good reputation, and be someone that people want to do business with without Noble Intent. You and your employees become better people and have a better quality of life. The bottom line is important, but it is not the ultimate measure of success."

White has had his share of Noble Intent skeptics. They listen to his speech about values and integrity and nod their heads in agreement. He knows that deep down some of those nodding heads are perched atop the bodies of hardened cynics. These skeptics have heard people talk the talk before but they have seen that the same people who speak of Noble Intent have failed to walk the walk when the time comes. They have noticed that profit often rules over integrity - that the numbers somehow make a difference when leaders have to make hard decisions about Noble Intent. Fortunately, Jim White talks the talk and walks the walk. Skeptics realize he is serious when they see their leader fire someone for flaunting the values on White's sheet of paper.

"Then they know we are serious," he said. "That is just what we believe in and this is our flag and this is what we will hold solid to. I believe in doing it by example and being consistent year in and year out. It works for me and it works for my organization and its people."

"Regard your neighbor's gain as your own gain, and your neighbor's loss as your own loss."

- *Taoism*, T'ai Shang Kan Ying P'ien

Chapter 20

Accountability & Noble Intent

In our interview with General Alexander we asked, "Do you think leadership notices when others are acting ignobly?"

General Alexander gave us an example that proved they do. He said that he was once on a self-directed team. Unfortunately, the time required for this task was substantial and the majority of the work had to be done after hours - 1630 to 2300. Others in the organization did not appreciate the goals of the team and this was exhibited in their behavior. They acted without Noble Intent, thwarting the team's efforts. They refused to provide information in a timely fashion, and generally made gathering information difficult. Lieutenant General Alexander's offices were far removed from the leadership center and he assumed that few people realized that the team was working so diligently almost every night. "I didn't know that they noticed how long and how late we were working. I also didn't know that they saw that the other group was giving us a hard time."

Leadership changed and the new leader asked several people about how the team worked. He wanted to understand the dynamics of his new organization. To General Alexander's surprise, he learned that a senior leader told the new leader that one group was trying to get a major tasking accomplished and another group was thwarting them. Thankfully, someone had the personal courage and the integrity to stand up and defend the team by saying, "One group is working day and night and the others are making it difficult for them to accomplish their responsibilities." The new leader said he would not tolerate that behavior. That honest feedback allowed the new leader to uncover the truth and call out people who were not behaving with Noble Intent.

General Alexander's story clearly shows how important information and leadership are in acting with Noble Intent. But individual leaders need to have the framework and institutional backing in order to make the Noble Intent message stick. This is true whether working in the private or public sectors, whether for the military or for non-profits. It is especially true when money is involved.

If there is anything in life Beverly Wright is sure of, it is this: First, making money is not a bad thing. The way you make it is what renders it good or bad. And second, most people have Noble Intent.

Wright learned those lessons early in a 30-year career that saw her rise to become the managing director of one investment banking firm and the chief financial officer of another. It was good fortune that her first jobs were with firms that not only preached what we now call Noble Intent, but insisted that employees practice it. "If you were going to work there, then you did the right thing," Wright said.

The top investment firms have always done what was ethically and financially best for client and company. Their reward for practicing Noble Intent has been longevity, profitability, and recognition as the industry's gold-standard.

"Many investment houses pride themselves for the number of years they have been in business," said Wright, whose employer had been in business since 1800 and has never had an unprofitable quarter. "You don't stay in business that long if you are not doing right by your clients."

Three decades ago, what constituted the "right thing" was fairly black and white. Today, however, some business people have distorted the concept. They have twisted doing the "right thing" to mean what is best for them at the expense of the client and firm. There are the obvious big name cases, such as Enron. But ethical lapses, and to a greater degree a "me first" attitude, have spread across the corporate landscape like an insidious virus. The only reliable vaccine, Wright believes, is Noble Intent.

"Noble Intent is strategically sound and, though it may not be popular and you may not want to hear it, it is viewed as the right way to operate a business profitably," said Wright. "Most people, if you look on a percentage basis, are saying it is good business for me to behave nobly. It is just smart. You can only fool an investor a couple of times before they say, `Thanks, but if your name is on the offering, no thanks.'"

But simply directing employees to practice Noble Intent is not enough. Employers, Wright said, must reinforce the concept by clearly defining its business standards. And then they must repeat it and repeat it and repeat it. In the corporate world, and especially in investment banking, a single employee's mistake can lead to big trouble.

"You can't allow someone to think Noble Intent is as easy as applying their objective measures," she said. "It is more complicated. So the senior guys have to essentially, every day, all day, articulate that this is how you make decisions. This is your framework for making decisions. You have to have this little rule book in your head."

Another firm Wright worked for dedicated hours to communicating its standards and rules to people who were literally making hundreds of Noble Intent-related decisions a week. The litmus test for whether an executive or employee had practiced Noble Intent in a given situation had a sort of "Old Testament environment" according to Wright. It came with punishments of biblical proportions, or at least punishments that fit the offense.

"If you did not want to stand up and tell the other partners about it, or you did not want to see it printed on the front page of the Wall Street Journal, then you were not supposed to do it," Wright said.

But, Wright admits, there are some people who just do not care about acting with or assuming Noble Intent. "Anyone who goes against this or openly flaunts the rules has to go," Wright said. "They may be a terrific talent, or a great money maker. But if they don't follow the established rules, they can cost the company in profit or, more important, reputation. The good news is that rule benders usually know they do not belong in a Noble Intent company and leave on their own. "You pretty much recognize when you are in a business which company practices each view," she said. "You have to look at your employer and make sure you are in the right place."

Chapter 21

Creating a Noble Intent-based World

For the past twenty-six years, Mark Victor Hansen has traveled the world helping countless people reshape their self-image and open doors to new opportunities and possibilities. He has reached another sixty million in North America alone through his books including, Cracking the Millionaire Code, and his mega best seller, Chicken Soup for the Soul.

What he has witnessed during his travels in the past few years has led Hansen to believe that the world is on the verge of a major change in which Noble Intent will play a key role.

"I think Noble Intent is going to catch on this decade," said Hansen, who also owns several businesses. "I think Noble Intent is different. It is a structural change. First of all, evolution-wise, it is time for it to happen. It is a fundamental change. It is a shift in the intelligence and a shift in global awareness. These are major changes that are going to happen fast."

His frequent visits to Africa and China have convinced Hansen that the structural shift is already underway. People in developing nations are beginning to understand and learn the business and economic principles that have sustained and contributed to the prosperity of the developed world. Some of those principles are so simple and rudimentary, like crop rotation, for instance, that we take them for granted. Another is the spread of electricity. Hansen's mentor, R. Buckminster Fuller, the American futurist, architect and philosopher, found that when electricity use goes up in an area, the population stabilizes. But people in poorer nations are only now being introduced to these concepts.

"The model isn't available to everyone," Hansen said. "You can't use a principle you have never heard of. People have to hear (about a principle) and be inspired by it. Inspiration is the ultimate calling."

The sole piece of the puzzle that is missing and necessary to launch this fundamental change, Hansen said, is what he calls the Solomon Principle. In biblical times, Hansen said, King Solomon used employment to keep peace and harmony among a disparate group of people. He hired everyone, regardless of race, color, or religious belief. Everyone prospered. Happy people, busy people, have no time and little inclination to fight.

"Right now there is no business Solomon," he said. "Perhaps he or she exists and is looming, about to come on the scene. Perhaps they just can't get the media coverage that puts them in the spotlight. The spirit laws of the universe say that this person or way of thinking shows up just in the nick of time. Nature is so efficient. It rains in April and you have food in the summer." Until "Solomon" arrives, Hansen is asking America's ten million millionaires to give away $1 million each.

"America is the greatest country because we are the givingest country," he said. "You can only be generous if you come from a mindset of abundance."

Hansen lauds those who have stepped up to the challenge. He cites people like Microsoft founder Bill Gates and his Bill Gates' Foundation, and fellow billionaire Warren Buffet, who donated $37 billion to the foundation.

"That is Noble Intent," he said. "Bill Gates and Warren Buffet have sent a powerful message and a lot of people are waking up. Why do you need all that money? No one can use it all. Sooner of later you wake up and say, 'One more suit does not make me any happier. I want to do stuff that has never been done before. But most important, I want to make a difference and help people. I want to do my best to make the world a better place."

Hansen saves his highest accolades for actor-philanthropist Paul Newman. In 1982 the star created Newman's Own to market his salad dressing and other all-natural products, including pasta sauces, salsa, popcorn, and steak sauce. From Day 1, Newman has donated 100 percent of the after-tax profits from the company to more than 1,000 charities. That comes to $200 million, according to the Newman's Own website. "That is visionary Noble Intent," Hansen said.

Fuller was the visionary who inspired Hansen to spend a lifetime helping others. "His Noble Intent was to make the world work for 100 percent

"That nature alone is good which refrains from doing unto another whatsoever is not good for itself."

- *Zoroastrianism*, Dadistan-i-dinik 94:5

of humanity, which is a wonderful Noble Intent," Hansen said. "I was inspired and uplifted."

Hansen said you do not have to be a Newman, Gates or Buffet to make the world a better place. In fact, you do not even have to be a millionaire. All you have to do is practice Noble Intent - which does not cost a penny.

"If we got every adult American to get into Noble Intent we can make the world work," he said. "When people hear the logic, they go, 'Yeah, I can buy that.'"

"And as ye would that men should do to you, do ye also to them likewise."

- Christianity
Luke 6:31, King James Version.